100 BEST
JEWISH RECIPES

100 BEST JEWISH RECIPES

TRADITIONAL AND CONTEMPORARY KOSHER
CUISINE FROM AROUND THE WORLD

Interlink Books

An imprint of Interlink Publishing Group, Inc.
Northampton, Massachusetts

CONTENTS

FOREWORD

Every cook I know has their go-to recipes—a handful of tried, trusted, and much-loved dishes that always work and never fail to delight. Fans of Evelyn Rose, the doyenne of Jewish cooking for over half a century, are no exception. In virtually every copy of the classic *New Complete International Jewish Cookbook*, there are certain pages where these well-thumbed books naturally fall open to reveal the tell-tale signs of their owner's "greatest hits": a pink beet stain beside Borscht on the Rocks, a trace of red wine in the margin of Florentine Beef Stew, or a buttery finger-mark over the method for Luscious Lemon Cake.

This new volume represents one hundred of Evelyn Rose's own best-loved recipes. With over a thousand recipes in *The New Complete* alone, choosing just one in ten was no mean feat, but this selection represent not only some of her personal favorites—as well as those of her fans—but her conviction that Jewish food is a living, evolving cuisine, rooted in tradition, but inspired by the present, just as it has been for centuries.

For Evelyn Rose, drawing inspiration from the tastes and ingredients of foreign lands, incorporating current thinking on health and nutrition, and using new technology to save time and effort, are the keys to modern Jewish cooking and to securing its future with new generations of cooking enthusiasts.

The recipes in this new collection, from Syrian Cheese Puffs to Gefilte Fish Provençale, epitomize these principles in addition to Evelyn's eclectic and adventurous approach to bringing new flavors to the Jewish table. In fact, whenever she was asked for a definition of Jewish food, her answer was simple: "It's food that Jews eat," wherever they might live or hail from.

Whether the recipe's heritage is haimische, Sephardi, Mediterranean, or Asian, my mother passionately believed that each dish must have *ta'am*—that extra something that makes it taste special, and so worth the effort for busy people to put on their table. She tested and fine-tuned each dish time and time again to ensure success for the home cook. This guarantee of fabulous food and recipes that "always work" is doubtless the reason why Evelyn's Rose's definitive work, *The Complete International Jewish Cookbook*, later revised by my mother and me, has been continuously in print since it was first published in 1976, and why her fans refer to it as their "bible."

When my mother wrote these recipes she also added her zest for life, a taste for adventure, and her own unique qualities: devotion to her craft, commitment to her readers, and an extra ingredient of her own—a large helping of love, all made possible by the support of her companion, taste-taster and greatest fan of all, her husband, Myer. Within these pages, you will find all this—and more—in generous measure. Enjoy.

Judi Rose

INTRODUCTION

ORIGINS

You can almost pinpoint the exact occasion, in the second millennium BCE, when the art of Jewish cooking was born. On that day, the course of world history was changed when the matriarch Rebecca, by the judicious use of herbs and spices, gave the savor of wild venison to the insipid flesh of a young kid, and established a culinary philosophy of "taste with economy" that has been followed by her descendants ever since.

When Rebecca made her kid casserole and her son Esau sold his birthright for a bowl of lentil soup, the everyday food of those early Jews was primitive in the extreme. Except on special occasions, the staple diet consisted of boiled vegetables—such as leeks, garlic, and onions—and salads of raw herbs, with boiled meat cooked only on a holiday. During the following 2,000 years, the Jews became in turn the subjects of the four civilizations in which the art of the kitchen was first evolved. When the empires of the Egyptians, Persians, Greeks, and Romans had faded into history, their cooking methods survived—in the kitchens of their former subjects.

To this day, Jewish households, during Pesach (the Feast of the Passover, see page 15), make a sweetmeat of dried apricots that their ancestors learned about when they were slaves in Egypt; they make a stuffed strudel with the same filling of poppyseeds and honey that was used to garnish the fattened dormice at Trimalchio's famous Roman feast; and during Shavuot (the Feast of Weeks, see page 15) they bake honey and cheese cakes that are a legacy of the many years of Seleucid rule.

If these "remembrances of foods past" were the sum total of Jewish cooking, it is doubtful that it would have survived to the present day. Jewish tradition teaches that when Moses descended from Mount Sinai he gave the Jews the code of culinary practice by which they have conducted their kitchens ever since, and which has been responsible, to a large extent, for the flavor and character of their food.

In the Jewish dietary laws, there are prohibitions: no shellfish; no pig; no carrion; no birds of prey; no thing that crawls upon its belly. Then there are the categories of permitted foods: only those fish that have fins and scales; only those beasts that chew the cud and have cloven hooves; only those birds that have been slaughtered according to the Law. Then there are the cooking and serving instructions for these permitted foods: foods of animal and dairy origin are not

to be combined, either during the cooking or the serving; dairy foods are to be served after meat foods only when a specified number of hours has elapsed; meat is to be purged of its blood before use.

However, it was instructions appearing in the Ten Commandments that have resulted in the development of some of the most typical of Jewish foods—those dishes that can be cooked one day and served the next. "On the seventh day thou shalt do no work, neither thy maidservant nor thy manservant," said the Law, and so all day Thursday, and most of Friday before dusk would be spent making salads, liver pâté, soups, fruit pies, yeast cakes, and, in particular, those meat and vegetable casseroles that could be left in a low oven overnight, such as Cholent and Tsimmes.

The need to differentiate between meat and milk meals encouraged the development of many delicious dairy dishes made from velvety kaese, a soft cheese made from naturally soured milk. These dishes include cheese kreplach (a form of ravioli), lokshen and kaese (noodle and cheese casserole), and the blintz, a paper-thin pancake stuffed with slightly sweetened cream cheese, which is possibly the most famous Jewish dish to be absorbed into international cuisine.

The shortage of kosher meat in the ghettos of medieval Europe forced households to find ways of stretching their meager supply. Usually, meat would be ground and used as a stuffing for a variety of different doughs and vegetables.

Those Jews who lived in the Middle East stuffed carrots, eggplants, tomatoes, and even leeks, using an ingenious metal "excavator" to remove the vegetable flesh from the skin. When meat became more plentiful, other methods of cooking it were adopted, but all were based on braising or casseroling, since kosher meat is used only a few days after it has been killed and tends to be tough when it is dry-roasted.

Some of the most interesting Jewish foods are those cooked in celebration of festivals (see pages 12–15). In biblical times, these festivals were the occasions for the family to make a pilgrimage on foot to the Temple at Jerusalem, where they would offer the first ripe fruits from their fields, as well as bread and cakes made from the new season's wheat.

No artificial leavening may be used in Pesach baking, so whisked sponges and meringues are the most popular confectionery. Since ordinary flour may not be used, ground nuts, matzo meal, and potato starch are substituted. There are almond macaroons, whisked sponge cakes and ground-nut torten, and cinnamon balls made of ground almonds and sugar; many of these are made from recipes dating back to the Middle Ages.

Perhaps the finest Jewish cooks of Western Europe were those who lived in the old Austro-Hungarian Empire. To these women, Friday was "strudel day"; they would rise at 6 a.m. to stretch the tissue-paper-thin dough onto a cloth laid on the kitchen table and then make meter-wide pans of yeast cake, topped with cherries (kirschen kuchen), plums (zwetschen kuchen), or cheese (kaese kuchen), which would last the family until after the Sabbath on the following day.

The cooking that is done in the majority of Western Jewish households, however, owes much of its inspiration to the fish and fowl of Poland, the Czech Republic, Slovakia, and the states that border the Baltic Sea. In the freshwater lakes of these countries swam the carp and the bream that were used to make the famous gefilte fish. Today, Western Jews use haddock, hake, cod, and halibut to make this delicious fish dish, which has a close affinity to the quenelles de brochet of France. If you visit Israel, you will have this mixture served in a pepper and tomato sauce, or as an appetizer, formed into little balls that are fried and served with pickled cucumbers. Gefilte fish apart, the new generations of Israeli Jews have discarded many of the traditional dishes of those families who came from the colder lands of Europe, and now enjoy a far lighter diet of vegetables, dairy, and fish, spiced with many traditional dishes of the Middle East.

Food of an entirely different nature from that prepared by Western Jews is cooked by those Jews who were expelled from Spain by Ferdinand and Isabella in 1492 and settled in many of the countries bordering the Mediterranean. The cookery of the Sephardim, as they are known, is spicy and aromatic, and their cakes, flavored with rosewater and almond oil, seem to have come straight out of the Arabian Nights.

THE RECIPES

Jewish food is no stranger to innovation—how else could it have survived as a recognizable cuisine through so many vicissitudes of fortune? The dishes in this book have come from a wide variety of Jewish communities across the globe. Some are traditional in the sense that they have been passed down through several generations. Others, however, are even now being absorbed into Jewish food culture. This enrichment of our cuisine has been going on for centuries and is one reason for its survival. The recipes in this book reflect the excitement, variety, flavor, history, and the love that is interwoven in what we call "Jewish food," and I hope that it will in some small way help to preserve it for generations to come.

FESTIVALS AND FOOD

The Jewish year follows the Lunar calendar, so the date of each festival in the Western (Gregorian) calendar varies from year to year.

ROSH HASHANAH
NEW YEAR
1 and 2 Tishri
(September/October)

Ever since the return from Babylon, where the art of sugar cooking is thought to have originated, Jewish households have made all kinds of sweet foods at this festival as a symbol of the sweetness they hope for in the year ahead. This sweetness is often introduced into dishes by using dried fruits or honey. While all kinds of fruit are served at Rosh Hashanah, the apple is the symbolic fruit of the season, expressing in both its sweetness and its round shape the hope for a satisfying and sweet New Year. As at every other festival, no Rosh Hashanah is complete without a platter of fried gefilte fish (see page 94).

YOM KIPPUR
THE DAY OF ATONEMENT
10 Tishri
(September/October)

At Yom Kippur, the Jewish people seek to atone for the sins between themselves and God. Although it is a Fast Day, the main preparations for the cook are concerned with making two special meals—that before the Fast on Kol Nidre (the eve of Yom Kippur), and that eaten 25 hours later, when it has ended. Simple, soothing food that is satisfying without being thirst-making is essential for Kol Nidre night. Chicken soup with kreplach or matzo balls, followed by an uncomplicated roast or braised bird, and a fruity dessert, followed by a large glass of lemon tea, is the general Ashkenazi pattern. After the meal, the table is cleared and then reset with the cloth and candles. After the Fast in Ashkenazi households, there are only minor variations from the sequence of the meal: a glass of Kiddush wine, then a piece of buttered kuchen or plain cake, with several cups of tea and some kind of smoked or pickled fish—some say it's to restore mineral salts lost by the body during the day, but most people enjoy the way a spiced food tickles the fasting palate—and then to the table for a fish meal and a not-too-demanding dessert.

SUKKOT
THE FEAST OF TABERNACLES
15 Tishri
(September/October)

Sukkot, the week-long autumn harvest festival commemorating the years that the Jews had to wander in the wilderness, living out their days in makeshift huts, is a particularly happy occasion in the Jewish calendar. Many families make their own Sukkah, or Tabernacle, where they eat their meals, and every house is sweet with the fragrance of fruit and flowers. Immediately after the end of the Yom Kippur Fast, it is the custom in many communities for the men to construct a Sukkah in the grounds of the synagogue, then line its roof—which must be partly open to the sky—with greenery. It is then decorated with fruit and vegetables—these are usually sent to hospitals and old people's homes at the end of the festival. At the end of each service, the congregation moves into the Sukkah for Kiddush (benediction) and a slice of a traditional cake or biscuit. To symbolize the richness of the harvest, stuffed foods of all kinds are served as both savories and sweets. Cabbages, vine leaves, tomatoes, and peppers are stuffed with lean ground beef and braised in a sweet-and-sour tomato or meat sauce. Known as holishkes and gevikelte kraut, these are the most popular in the West, but in Israel, stuffed eggplants are making a new tradition.

SIMCHAT TORAH
THE REJOICING
OF THE LAW
23 Tishri
(September/October)

The festival of Simchat Torah is the moment when the last portion of the Torah (the Five Books of Moses) is read in the synagogue, and the weekly readings from the Sefer Torah (the Scroll of the Law) start all over again with a passage from Beresheit (Genesis). It concludes the month of High Holy Days (September and October in the Western calendar). On Simchat Torah, all the Scrolls of the Law are taken from the Holy Ark—the holiest place in the synagogue in which they are stored—and paraded around the synagogue with much singing and dancing, in which the whole congregation joins. Children take advantage of the lack of the usual decorum to wave flags and pelt the readers with candies—which they immediately scramble to pick up. A special reception is held after the service either to honor the two "Bridegrooms of the Law," who have read the final and first portions of the Law, or just the Chatan Torah, while the other—the Chatan Beresheit—is honored on the following Saturday on Shabbat Beresheit. Either way, everyone enjoys delicious vegetable dips and luscious cakes.

CHANUKKAH
THE FEAST OF LIGHTS
25 Kislev
(December)

The famous defeat of the Greeks in the second century BCE by Judas Maccabaeus (in Hebrew, Yehuda HaMaccabee) and his followers is celebrated during the eight days of Chanukkah with parties and presents—particularly for children.

Tradition states that after Yehuda's family, the Hasmoneans, had been inspired by their father, Mattathias the High Priest, to defeat the tyrant Antiochus IV—who had desecrated the Temple in Jerusalem with pagan rites—there was only enough pure, undefiled oil for the sacred Menorah (seven-branched candelabra) for it to burn for 24 hours. By a miracle, the Menorah stayed alight for eight days and nights until more pure oil could be obtained.

So in every Jewish home, an extra candle is lit in the Chanukkah (the eight-branched candelabra) on each of the eight nights of Chanukkah, and the family and their friends gather around to sing the famous hymn of praise, "Maoz Tsur" ("Rock of Ages") as they celebrate the Miracle of the Oil. So it's not surprising that foods cooked in oil have become traditional at this festival, as well as rich and sweet foods such as trifles and fruit cakes.

PURIM
THE FEAST OF LOTS
14 Adar
(February/March)

Purim occurs exactly one month before Passover. It commemorates the downfall of Haman, the evil vizier of King Ahasuerus (Artaxerxes II), who in the fifth century BCE formulated his own Final Solution by planning the massacre of the entire Jewish population of Persia. According to the story, Haman drew lots to decide on which day to exterminate the Jews. However, he ended up on the gallows he had prepared for his enemies, and his notoriety is perpetuated in a variety of cakes and sweetmeats.

PESACH
PASSOVER
15 Nissan
(March/April)

Each spring, Passover, the great festival of freedom, commemorates the liberation of Jews from slavery in Egypt more than 3,500 years ago. This festival is seen as a time of renewal, a great family occasion, when everyone gathers to enjoy the Seder—the ceremonial meal. The order of the courses is laid down in the Haggadah, a text used by Jewry worldwide for centuries past. During the Seder meal, the story of the Exodus from Egypt is read from the Haggadah, and a succession of symbolic foods, displayed on a special plate, are tasted by everyone at the table. The kitchen is filled with the wonderful perfume of eingemacht (Passover preserves and lemon curd), and the cakes and cookies—the macaroons, sponge cakes, and cinnamon balls, whose recipes have been passed down the chain from mother to daughter since early medieval times—are ready and waiting for the family's verdict.

SHAVUOT
**PENTECOST OR
THE FEAST OF WEEKS**
6 Sivan
(May/June)

In earlier days, when the Temple still stood in Jerusalem, Shavuot was celebrated as a great agricultural festival, when the start of the wheat harvest was marked by offerings of newly baked bread. Every man brought the first fruits of his crops to the Temple, while his wife ground flour from the new season's wheat and baked special cakes and bread in honor of the occasion. Today Jewish people commemorate those early days by decorating the house with flowers and plants and by taking them as gifts to the synagogue. This festival also celebrates the giving of the Torah—the code of Jewish Law—to Moses on Mount Sinai. The Torah sets out the dietary laws—the regulations that relate to the preparation and consumption of food in the community. Another tradition links the custom to the gift of the land "flowing with milk and honey." So milk and foods derived from it have become the most famous symbolic foods of this festival.

These dairy ingredients are made into some of the most delicious dishes of Jewish cuisine—such as the cheesecakes and blintzes, and the kreplach and lokshen casseroles.

SMALL PLATES

CHATZILIM
"POOR MAN'S CAVIAR"

SERVES 4–6 AS AN APPETIZER, 8–10 AS A DIP
KEEPS FOR 2 WEEKS IN THE FRIDGE | DO NOT FREEZE

A delicious Eastern Mediterranean appetizer, particularly popular in Israel, chatzilim is served like a pâté with pita or toast and butter, or as a stuffing for tomatoes. It is also known as potljelly by Romanian Jews.

1 lb/450g eggplants

1 garlic clove, crushed

1 tbsp finely chopped onion

1 tbsp chopped parsley

1 tbsp chopped green pepper (optional)

1 tsp sea salt, or more to taste

10 grinds of black pepper, or more to taste

1 tbsp extra virgin olive oil

juice of ½ lemon, or more to taste

black olives and pita or challah (see page 140), to serve

Cut off the prickly stalk-ends of the eggplants, then prick all over with a fork—this prevents them bursting and burning the cook! Traditionally the eggplants are grilled over charcoal, giving the dish its characteristic smoky flavor. However, unless you have a charcoal grill on hand it's much more convenient to preheat the oven to 450°F/230°C and bake them 8–30 minutes until they have begun to collapse and a skewer meets no resistance when the center is pierced.

If more convenient, lay them on a paper towel and cook in the microwave until tender. Leave to stand for 1 minute, then pierce with a skewer to test as before. If you want a smoky flavor, char each softened eggplant by holding it briefly over the open flame of a gas stove (use barbecue tongs or a long-handled fork). Allow to cool for a few minutes, then cut in half and scoop out the flesh from the skin.

Chop the remaining ingredients into the eggplant flesh using a large cook's knife, mezzaluna, or hackmesser (an old-fashioned wooden-handled chopper), adding the olive oil and lemon juice last. Taste and add more lemon juice, salt, and pepper, if necessary.

Put into a shallow pottery dish. Garnish with black olives and serve with challah or warm pita bread.

HUMMUS B'TAHINA
WITH TOASTED PINE NUTS

SERVES 4–6, OR 15 WITH 2 OTHER DIPS
KEEPS FOR 3 DAYS IN THE FRIDGE | DO NOT FREEZE

1 small bunch of flat-leaf parsley

2 tbsp extra virgin olive oil

7oz/200g good-quality
ready-made hummus

1 ½ tbsp tahini

1 tbsp lemon juice

½ tsp ground cumin

2 tbsp pine nuts, toasted in a
dry pan

Process the parsley with the oil in a food processor until the oil is bright green and the parsley finely chopped. Put in a small bowl and set aside.

Process all the other ingredients except the pine nuts until evenly blended. Taste for seasoning, adding extra lemon juice if not tangy enough. Spoon into a fairly shallow dish. Just before serving, drizzle with the herbed oil and sprinkle with the pine nuts.

LIPTAUER CHEESE

SUFFICIENT TO TOP 60 SAVORY CRACKERS OR SLICES OF FRENCH BREAD
KEEPS FOR 1 WEEK IN THE FRIDGE | DO NOT FREEZE

This Viennese cream cheese dip has a deliciously piquant mix of flavors.

7oz/200g low-fat cream cheese

1 tsp anchovy paste, or 2 finely
chopped canned anchovies

2 tsp capers, rinsed and drained

1 tsp Dijon or English mustard

2 tsp paprika

a few twists of black pepper

celery salt (optional)

1 tbsp snipped chives

Beat all the ingredients together, then leave for several hours to develop the flavor.

CHEESE BLINTZES

SERVES 6 AS AN APPETIZER
FILLED BUT UNBROWNED BLINTZES KEEP FOR 1 DAY IN THE FRIDGE
UNFILLED PANCAKES FREEZE FOR 3 MONTHS, FILLED PANCAKES FREEZE FOR 1 MONTH

These are one of the glories of Jewish cuisine. The Yiddish word for these paper-thin pancakes is bletlach—or skeleton leaves—which gives some indication of how thin they should be.

FOR THE BATTER

1 cup/4oz/125g all-purpose flour

1 pinch of salt

2 large eggs

2–3 tbsp oil

½ cup/125ml milk

4–6 tbsp/2–3oz/60–80g butter

FOR THE FILLING

1½ cups/12oz/350g curd cheese or strained cottage cheese, mixed with 2 tbsp sour cream, yogurt, or fromage frais or 1 egg yolk (whichever is most convenient)

1 tsp sugar

1 pinch of salt

TO SERVE

ice-cold sour cream

Sift the flour and salt into a bowl. Make a well, drop in the eggs and 2 teaspoons of oil, and stir. Gradually mix in the milk and about ½ cup/125ml water until smooth. Whisk until the surface is covered with tiny bubbles. Set aside to rest for 30 minutes. To make the filling, mix all the ingredients together and set aside.

Stir the batter well and pour into a jug—it should be the consistency of light cream. Put a 6–7in/16–18cm diameter nonstick omelet pan over medium heat for 3 minutes, then drop in a teaspoonful of oil, and swirl it around the base and side of the pan. Wipe out any excess with a paper towel. Using a piece of paper towel, smear the entire inner surface of the pan very thinly with butter, then pour in a thick layer of batter, swirling it around so that it covers the side and base of the pan. The heat will immediately set a thin layer so that the excess can be poured back into the jug. The blintz should be so thin that by the time the sides begin to curl from the pan, the bottom will be brown and the top side dry. Turn the blintz out on to a sheet of wax paper. Repeat the process until all of the pancakes have been made. Stack the pancakes on top of each other, browned-side up.

To stuff, place a pancake brown-side up on your work surface. Spread a tablespoon of the filling thinly over the bottom half, turn in the sides, and roll into a long, thin roll. Repeat with each pancake. Heat 4 tablespoons/2oz/60g butter and 2 teaspoons of oil in a wide frying pan. The moment the butter stops foaming, put in the stuffed blintzes, join-side upwards. Cook gently for 3 minutes until golden brown, turn, and cook the second side. Serve with sour cream.

CHICKEN LIVER PÂTÉ JEWISH STYLE

SERVES 6 AS AN APPETIZER, 8–10 AS A SPREAD
KEEPS FOR 5 DAYS IN THE FRIDGE | FREEZES FOR 1 MONTH

The onion in this recipe is sautéed to caramelize it and enrich the flavor of this superb pâté. Using cooked rather than raw onion also helps the pâté keep for longer. This kind of liver pâté can be made with a grinder, but to get a smooth and "creamy" texture, it should be made in a food processor.

3 eggs (1 for the garnish)

1 onion, finely chopped

1 garlic clove, crushed

4 tbsp/2oz/60g soft margarine, butter, or rendered chicken fat

5–10 grinds of sea salt

12oz/350g ready-koshered chicken livers

15 grinds of black pepper

1 good pinch of freshly grated nutmeg

TO SERVE

warm French bread, crackers, or slices of challah (see page 140)

Hard-boil the eggs for 10 minutes, drain, then return to the pan, cover with cold water, and then leave to cool.

Fry the onion and the garlic gently in the margarine, butter, or fat until very soft and a rich brown (this is important if the right depth of flavor is to be achieved). As the onion cooks, sprinkle it with the sea salt.

Peel the eggs and cut them in half. Put 1 egg aside.

Put the onion and garlic with their cooking juices into the food processor and process until smooth, then add 2 eggs and all the remaining ingredients and process again until smooth. Taste and add more seasoning if necessary, but remember that the flavors will intensify over the next few hours.

Turn the mixture into a terrine or oval gratin dish or divide between individual ramekins. Chill, covered with plastic wrap, preferably overnight. Refrigerate the extra egg.

One hour before serving, remove the pâté from the fridge to return to room temperature. Just before serving, pass the remaining egg through a food mill or sieve and use it to decorate the top of the pâté. Serve with warm French bread, crackers, or slices of challah.

EGG AND SCALLION FORSPEISE

SERVES 6 AS AN APPETIZER, 15 AS A SPREAD
KEEPS FOR 1 DAY IN THE FRIDGE | DO NOT FREEZE

This delicious appetizer is traditionally made with a hackmesser, or wooden-handled chopper. In many families, this long and tedious job was performed by one of the men using a hackbrettle— a wooden chopping board with sides. A grinder produces entirely the wrong texture, but it can be made just as effectively with a food processor.

1 bunch of scallions, white parts and 4in/10cm of the green, or 1 onion, cut into 1in/2.5cm chunks

8 hard-boiled eggs, shelled and halved

4 tbsp/2oz/50g soft margarine, butter, rendered chicken fat, or chicken-flavored vegetable fat

½ tsp salt

10 grinds of black pepper

TO SERVE

warm French bread, crackers, or slices of challah (see page 140)

Put the onions into the bowl of a food processor and pulse for 3 seconds until roughly chopped. Add all the remaining ingredients and pulse for a further 5 seconds until finely chopped and blended.

Turn the mixture into a small gratin dish, smooth the top to level, and mark with a pattern using the blade of a knife. Cover and chill for at least an hour before serving.

Serve with warm French bread, crackers, or slices of challah.

OLD-FASHIONED
PICKLED HERRINGS

SERVES 6 | PICTURED ON PAGE 24
KEEPS FOR 6 WEEKS IN THE FRIDGE BUT BECOMES MORE ACIDIC WITH TIME

Sometimes called Bismarcks or rollmops, these can be bought in jars, but they are especially delicious if you make your own. If salt herrings are not available, soak 6 fresh, cleaned, and boned herrings in ¼ cup/2oz/50g salt and 2½ cups/575ml water for 2 hours, then continue as below.

3 salt herrings

white pepper

I onion, thinly sliced into rings

I large unpeeled lemon, sliced

I tbsp pickling spice

2 bay leaves

I dried chili pepper

2½ cups/575ml white vinegar

2½ tbsp brown sugar

Behead the herrings, slit the belly, and remove the entrails. Put the fish in a glass casserole dish (so that the smell will not linger) and place under the cold-water faucet. Leave the water running in a gentle trickle. After 15 minutes, turn off the water and let the herrings stand overnight covered in cold water.

The next day, lift the fish out of the water and drain well. Lay them on a piece of newspaper or paper towel, hold the tail firmly, and scrape from the tail to the head with a blunt knife to remove loose scales. Wash again in cold water and put the fish on a board. Open the front, turn the fish over, and press the back with the flat of your hand. Turn over again and the backbone will lift out easily. Remove the tails if you prefer, and any other loose bones.

Sprinkle each herring very lightly with white pepper, add 2–3 thin rings of onion, then roll up from tail to head. If the herrings are large, you may find it easier to split them lengthways before rolling. Skewer them closed with wooden toothpicks. Put them in a glass jar in alternate layers with the lemon, onion, and spices.

Put the vinegar and sugar into a pan and bring to a boil, then immediately turn off the heat and leave until it is lukewarm. Pour this over the herrings. Cover and refrigerate for 4 days before using.

Serve in ½in/1.25cm slices, either speared on a toothpick or as an hors d'oeuvre, garnished with the pickled onion slices.

HAIMISCHE PICKLED CUCUMBERS

MAKES 11 LB/5KG | PICTURED ON PAGE 25
KEEPS FOR 4–6 WEEKS IN THE FRIDGE

Pickled cucumbers are known as ugekes in Yiddish, and this recipe is the most delicious version of the pickle that I know—it originates from Lithuania and the name haimische means comfort food. The cucumbers are traditionally pickled a month before Rosh Hashana (New Year), so that they provide a special, homey treat for the holiday.

½ cup/4oz/100g coarse or kosher salt

2¼lb/1kg firm green gherkins or ridge cucumbers 4–6 in/ 10–15cm long

FOR THE PICKLING SOLUTION

1 piece of dried ginger root

2 red pickling chilies

2 garlic cloves

1 tbsp mixed pickling spice

2 bay leaves

1 tbsp distilled malt vinegar

Put 8 cups/2l water into a large pan with the salt and pickling solution ingredients. Bring to a boil, stirring until the salt has dissolved. Boil rapidly for 5 minutes. Take off the heat and leave until absolutely cold.

Scrub the cucumbers thoroughly with a small soft-bristle nailbrush (kept especially for the purpose), discarding any that have soft or damaged parts. Rinse them in cold water, then layer in a large bowl. As each layer is put in the bowl, scatter over some of the spices fished out from the liquid.

Cover the cucumbers with a large upturned plate, then weigh down with something heavy, such as a couple of full food cans wrapped in a plastic bag. Pour the cold pickling solution down the side of the bowl until it covers the plate to a depth of 1in/2.5cm. Cover with cheesecloth or a thin dish towel and leave in a very cool place for 10 days.

After 10 days, skim the froth from the surface. Cover again and leave for a further week.

Skim again, and test by slicing into a cucumber. If the taste is not right—it should be salty and slightly sour—leave them for a further week, or until ready. Skim again, pack into large sterilized glass containers, and fill up with the pickling liquid until the cucumbers are completely submerged. Store in the fridge.

SYRIAN CHEESE PUFFS

MAKES ABOUT 25 CHEESE PUFFS
MAKE AND BAKE THE SAME DAY | DO NOT REHEAT

Because of the separation of meat and milk foods laid down in the dietary laws, Jewish cooking has always put special emphasis on dairy dishes. These delicious little bites, also known as savory Sephardi cheesecakes, can be served as a main course for a dairy lunch or with drinks. They are always a hit at parties.

7oz/200g mature or extra-mature Cheddar cheese

1 large egg

½ tsp salt, less if the cheese is salty

1 lb 2oz/500g puff pastry

2 tbsp sesame seeds

Cut the cheese into pieces that will fit into the feed tube of your food processor, then wrap in plastic wrap and freeze for 1 hour—this stops the cheese from melting and gumming up the mechanism when you grate it. Grate the cheese using the fine grater disc, then transfer to a large bowl.

Preheat the oven to 425°F/220°C and line two large baking trays with parchment paper. Whisk the egg to blend, setting 1 tablespoon aside for glazing the puffs. Add the the salt and cheese to the whisked egg and mix to a sticky paste.

Roll the pastry to the thickness of a knife blade, then cut with a 2½in/6cm cookie cutter or glass rim into about 25 rounds. Alternatively, cut into 2½in/6cm squares.

Dampen the edges of each piece, place a teaspoon of filling in the center, and fold over to form a half moon (or triangle if you are working with squares). Seal firmly with the tines of a fork. Arrange on the prepared baking trays. Brush with the reserved beaten egg, then dip the brushed side in a bowl of sesame seeds to coat. Bake for 10–15 minutes until crisp and golden. Serve warm.

COCKTAIL FISH BALLS

SERVES 4–6 (MAKES 30 SMALL BALLS)
KEEP FOR 1 DAY IN THE FRIDGE | FREEZE FOR 3 MONTHS

FOR THE FISH MIX

1 lb 2oz/500g fish fillet (a mixture of haddock and cod)

1 tsp salt, plus extra to salt the fish

½ onion, cut into chunks

1 large egg

5 grinds of black pepper

1 tsp sugar

1 tbsp oil

¼ cup/3oz/30g medium matzo meal, plus extra, if needed

FOR THE COATING

½ cup/2oz/60g medium matzo meal

oil for deep-frying

TO SERVE

tartar sauce (see page 180)

Wash and salt the fish and set aside to drain. Put the onion in a food processor with the egg, salt, pepper, sugar, and oil and process to a smooth purée. Transfer to a bowl, stir in the matzo meal, then leave to swell.

Working in batches, process the fish in the processor for 5 seconds until finely chopped, then add to the onion purée and blend in using a large fork. The mixture should be firm enough to shape into a soft patty or ball. If it feels too "cloggy," rinse out the processor bowl with 1 or 2 tablespoons of water and stir that in. If it feels very soft, stir in 1 or 2 tablespoons more matzo meal. Leave for half an hour, or overnight in the fridge, if preferred.

Use a small ice cream scoop to portion out the mixture, or partially fill a large pastry bag without a nozzle and pipe out in blobs the size of a walnut. Roll between your palms into little balls.

Put half of the balls into a large plastic bag with half of the matzo meal. Shake until the balls are evenly coated. Repeat with the rest of the balls and meal.

Heat the oil to 360°F/180°C, or hot enough to brown a 1in/2.5cm cube of bread in 40 seconds. Deep-fry the balls in batches until golden brown, then drain on crumpled paper towels or a cooling rack set over a baking tray and leave to cool.

Serve or freeze for later use: place the cooled balls into plastic bags and freeze until required. To serve, spread the frozen balls onto an oven tray and heat at 350°F/180°C until crisp—about 5 minutes. Serve warm or cold, speared on cocktail sticks, with chrane (horseradish and beet relish) or tartar sauce (see page 180).

SOUPS

TRADITIONAL CHICKEN SOUP

SERVES 4–6

KEEPS FOR 3 DAYS IN THE FRIDGE | FREEZES FOR 3 MONTHS

Chicken soup is traditionally made by simmering a whole bird with the giblets in water flavored with a variety of vegetables. However, the soup can be made with just the wings and giblets, and the flavor strengthened using a chicken bouillon cube.

I whole or half chicken or stewing hen, including wings and giblets (excluding livers)

2 tsp salt

I pinch of white pepper

I large onion

2 large carrots

leaves and top 2in/5cm of 2 celery stalks

I sprig of parsley

I very ripe tomato

TO SERVE

knaidlach (matzo balls, see page 178) or lokshen, vermicelli, or egg noodles (about ¼ cup/½oz/15g per person, cooked according to package instructions)

Put the bird, wings, and giblets in a large, heavy soup pot with 7½ cups/ 1.75l water, and the salt and pepper (the feet would traditionally be added at this stage too). Cover and bring to a boil. Remove any foam with a large, wet metal spoon.

Peel the onion and carrots, cut in half, and add to the pan with celery, parsley, and tomato. Bring back to a boil, then reduce the heat so that the liquid is barely bubbling. Cover and continue to simmer for a further 3 hours, either on top of the stove or in a slow oven at 300°F/150°C, or until the chicken feels very tender when a leg is prodded.

Strain the soup into a large bowl, reserving the giblets and carrots in a separate container. Pour off the fat in batches using a large fat separator. Alternatively, cover the pot and place it in the fridge overnight. The next day, remove any congealed fat and return the soup to the pan. (If there is a thick layer of fat, it can be heated in a pan to drive off any liquid and then, when it has stopped bubbling, cooled and stored like rendered raw fat.)

Finely cube the cooked giblets and the carrots. Add these to the soup with the knaidlach, lokshen, vermicelli, or egg noodles. Reheat gently before serving.

CHICKEN SOUP—3 WAYS

ALL RECIPES SERVE 4
KEEP FOR 3 DAYS IN THE FRIDGE | FREEZE FOR 3 MONTHS

The basis of these three soups is a completely defatted chicken stock with a selection of cubed vegetables and a little optional vermicelli. Although ideal for slimmers, they are delicious enough to serve to non-dieters as well.

To defat the chicken stock quickly and completely, partly freeze it for 2–3 hours until the fat is solid enough to scrape off with a spoon. If you like a thicker soup, you may prefer the zucchini and lettuce version opposite. All three soups will improve if left for at least 6 hours before serving. Reheat gently until bubbling.

CHICKEN NOODLE SOUP

5 cups/1.2l homemade (see page 176), or best-quality bought chicken stock

3oz/75g white part of a leek, cubed

3oz/75g carrots, shredded

3oz/75g yellow pepper, deseeded and shredded

1 nest uncooked vermicelli pasta

salt and ground black pepper, to taste

2 tsp chopped parsley

Bring the stock to a boil, add the cubed vegetables and the vermicelli, cover, and simmer for 10 minutes. Taste and add salt and pepper, if necessary. Add the parsley just before serving.

CHICKEN, ZUCCHINI, AND LETTUCE SOUP

1 1/2 lb/680g zucchinis, unpeeled, thinly sliced

1 tbsp finely minced dried onion (optional)

5 cups/1.2l homemade (see page 176), or best-quality bought chicken stock

1/2 tsp salt

15 grinds of black pepper

1 head of lettuce, shredded

2 tsp chopped parsley or snipped chives

Put the zucchinis, onion (if using), stock, salt, and pepper into a soup pot and simmer, covered, until the zucchinis are soft— 10-15 minutes. Add the shredded lettuce and let the soup bubble, uncovered, for 3 minutes. Blend or process until smooth. Just before serving, stir in the parsley or chives.

CHICKEN, MUSHROOM, AND ZUCCHINI SOUP

5 cups/1.2l homemade (see page 176), or best-quality bought chicken stock

1 1/2 cups/4 1/2 oz/125g very fresh mushrooms with stalks, wiped with a damp cloth, then thinly sliced

1 large carrot, cut into 1/2 in/1 cm cubes

1 zucchini, cut into 1/2 in/1 cm slices

2 tsp tomato paste

salt and ground black pepper, to taste

2 tsp chopped parsley

Bring the stock to a boil, add the mushrooms, carrot, and zucchini. Stir in the tomato paste, then cover and simmer for 10 minutes. Taste and add salt and pepper, if necessary. Add the parsley just before serving.

MOTHER'S MILCHIKE SOUP

SERVES 6

KEEPS FOR 3 DAYS IN THE FRIDGE | FREEZES FOR 3 MONTHS

This soup was made to herald summer in the villages of the Pale of Settlement, in Russia. It is fresh and simple, with the flavor of young vegetables. Some families make tiny knaidlach (see page 178), made with butter instead of chicken fat, and serve them in this soup.

3 tbsp/1 ½oz/40g butter

1 onion, finely chopped

4 baby potatoes, cubed

1 carrot, grated

1 lb/450g fresh or frozen mixed vegetables (including baby carrots and petit pois or peas)

1 tsp salt

1 pinch of black pepper

1 tsp sugar

1 tbsp cornstarch

1 ¼ cups/275ml milk

1 tbsp snipped chives or scallion tops

Melt the butter in a heavy pan and sweat the onion in the covered pan until soft and golden. Add the potatoes, carrot, and mixed vegetables. Cover with 3¾ cups/850ml water and add the salt, pepper, and sugar. Simmer, covered, for 30 minutes, or until all the vegetables are tender.

Mix the cornstarch into the milk, then stir it into the soup and simmer, still stirring, for 3 minutes. Stir in the chives or scallion tops.

HOBENE GROPEN
BEEF SOUP WITH OATS

SERVES 4
KEEPS FOR 3 DAYS IN THE FRIDGE | FREEZES FOR 3 MONTHS

This is a creamy-textured soup that is especially rich in the B vitamins. It is made with a type of oat known in Jewish households as hobene gropen or hubergrits, but also called Irish or steel-cut oats. Because it is a whole-grain cereal, it does need to be simmered for several hours, but the result is a wonderfully sustaining winter soup.

3 tbsp hobene gropen (steel-cut oats)

½lb/225g or more beef shank

1 tsp salt, or more to taste

½ tsp white pepper, or more to taste

4¼ cups/1l meat stock (see page 177)

1 large potato

1 onion

1 carrot

1 fat celery stalk

1 good sprig of parsley, plus extra chopped parsley, to serve

Put the hobene gropen into a small bowl, cover with boiling water, and leave to settle while you add the beef, with the salt and pepper, to the stock. Bring to a boil and skim off any foam with a metal spoon. Add the strained hobene gropen, reduce the heat so that the soup is barely bubbling, then cover and simmer in this way for 1 hour.

Meanwhile, cut the potato into ½in/1.25cm cubes, and cube the onion, carrot, and celery into ¼in/5mm cubes. Add these vegetables to the soup, together with the parsley sprig. Cover again and simmer for a further 2 hours, by which time the soup should be creamy and the meat tender. Remove the parsley sprig, taste the soup, and add more salt and pepper, if required. Sprinkle with chopped parsley and serve piping hot.

To serve on the second day, add half a cup of water and reheat gently.

HAIMISCHE WINTER SOUP

SERVES 4

KEEPS FOR 3 DAYS IN THE FRIDGE | FREEZES FOR 3 MONTHS

Haimische can be roughly translated as comfort food, so this is par excellence the soup "like Mama used to make." Indeed, for nineteenth-century Russian and Polish peasants, it was also a main dish of the day, as the legumes and cereals it contained made it extremely nourishing, while still cheap. The consistency of the soup can also be easily adjusted by boiling it down or diluting it with extra stock.

I cup/4oz/100g green split peas

¼ cup/2¼oz/60g red lentils

2 tbsp pearl barley

3 tbsp navy beans

½lb/225g soup meat such as beef shank (optional)

4¼ cups/1l homemade stock (see page 176), or 7½ cups/1.75l water and I soup bone

I tsp salt

5 grinds of black pepper

I tsp fines herbes (or a mixture of dried parsley, chives, tarragon, and chervil)

I large sprig of parsley

2 large carrots, I cut into ½in/1cm cubes, and I grated

I celery stalk, cut into ¾in/2cm cubes

white part of a fat leek, well washed and thinly sliced

I tbsp tomato paste (optional)

The day before making the soup, put the split peas, lentils, barley, and navy beans into a large bowl, cover with twice their depth of cold water, and leave to soak and swell overnight.

The next day, put the meat and the stock (or the water and bone) with the salt into a large soup pot and bring to a boil. Skim off any foam with a wet metal spoon. Tip the legumes and barley into a fine sieve to remove any excess soaking water, then rinse thoroughly under cold running water until the water that drains from them is quite clear.

Add to the soup pot with the black pepper and herbs and all the vegetables except the grated carrot. Bring back to a boil, then reduce the heat until the mixture is barely bubbling. Cover and simmer for 2 hours, then uncover and add the grated carrot. Continue to cook for a further I hour, stirring the pan occasionally to make sure the soup does not stick to the base of the pot as it thickens. The soup is ready when the lentils and split peas have turned into a purée. Taste and add more seasoning, if required. Remove the sprig of parsley before serving.

Before reheating leftover soup, you can add I tablespoon of tomato paste mixed with ½ cup/120ml water to thin it down.

BORSCHT ON THE ROCKS

SERVES 6
COOKED BEET JUICE KEEPS FOR 4 DAYS IN THE FRIDGE, COMPLETE SOUP FOR 2 DAYS
FREEZES FOR 3 MONTHS

A chilled glass of that heart-of-winter favorite, beet borscht, makes a superb non-alcoholic aperitif to a summer dairy lunch. If you prefer, you can serve a larger quantity as a cold appetizer for the meal. Calories can be trimmed by substituting Greek yogurt or fromage frais for the more traditional sour cream.

1 lb 5oz/600g beets

1 onion

1 carrot

4¼ cups/1 l hot water plus 2 vegetable bouillon cubes

10 grinds of black pepper

1 tbsp sugar

TO THICKEN

2 tbsp lemon juice

2 eggs

scant ½ cup/100ml sour cream, Greek yogurt, or creamy fromage frais

Have a large saucepan ready. Trim the beets, wash thoroughly, and peel if old. Peel the onion and the carrot. Cut all the vegetables into roughly 1 in/2.5cm chunks, then process in two batches until very finely chopped. Place in the pan with the water, pepper, and sugar. Bring to a boil, cover, and simmer for 20 minutes until the vegetables are soft and the liquid is a rich, dark red.

Pour the contents through a coarse strainer into a bowl and discard the vegetables. Return the strained juice to the pan and leave on low heat. Put the lemon juice and eggs into the food processor and process for 5 seconds until well mixed. With the motor running, pour two ladles of the hot juice through the feed tube and process for a further 3 seconds, then add to the rest of the juice in the pan and heat gently, whisking constantly until the soup is steaming and has thickened slightly. Do not let it boil or it will curdle. Taste and adjust the seasoning, if necessary, so that there is a gentle blend of sweet and sour.

Cool, then chill thoroughly. Just before serving, whisk in the cream, yogurt, or fromage frais.

TARATOUR
HERBED YOGURT AND CUCUMBER SOUP

SERVES 6
KEEPS FOR 3 DAYS IN THE FRIDGE | DO NOT FREEZE

The herbs can be from the garden or the supermarket but use them fresh rather than dried for this delicate summer soup. Smetana is an Eastern European sour cream— you can use sour cream, Greek yogurt, or crème fraîche if you cannot obtain it.

1 ¼ cups/275ml 2% milk

2 cups/425ml plain yogurt

⅔ cup/150ml smetana (or substitute sour cream, Greek yogurt, or crème fraîche)

1 cucumber

1 small bunch of radishes

2 tbsp snipped chives

2 heaped tbsp dill leaves, or 1 heaped tbsp chopped parsley

2 sprigs of tarragon, chopped

1 small bunch of very fresh, young mint, chopped

½ tsp salt

10 grinds of black pepper

In a large jug or lipped bowl, gently stir together the milk, yogurt, and smetana (or substitute).

Peel the cucumber and cut it into matchsticks. Trim the radishes and slice very thinly. Prepare the herbs.

Stir all of these into the yogurt mixture, together with the salt and pepper. Cover, and refrigerate until well chilled. Stir before serving.

SOUPE AU CRESSON
WATERCRESS SOUP

SERVES 6
KEEPS FOR 2 DAYS IN THE FRIDGE | PURÉE FREEZES FOR 2 MONTHS

The slightly acidic, tangy taste of watercress is especially delicious in a cold soup but equally good when hot. You can use less, but the three bunches suggested do produce a soup to remember.

9oz/250g watercress (about 3 small bunches)

3 tbsp/1½oz/40g butter

1 onion, finely chopped

white part of 1 fat leek, finely sliced

1 lb/450g potatoes, thinly sliced

5 cups/1.2l vegetable stock

1 bay leaf

1½–2 tsp salt

15 grinds of black pepper

1¼ cups/275ml milk

TO SERVE

leaves from reserved watercress, finely chopped

⅔ cup/150ml sour cream or plain Greek yogurt

2½ tbsp pine nuts or sliced almonds, toasted in a dry pan

Wash and spin-dry all the watercress in 3 batches, then cut off the leaves from one bunch and set them aside in the refrigerator, wrapped carefully.

Melt the butter in a soup pot, add the onion and leek, and sauté, covered, for 2 minutes until soft and golden. Add the potatoes, stock, bay leaf, salt, and pepper, bring to a boil, cover, and simmer for 20 minutes until the potatoes are tender. Add the remaining watercress, stalks as well as leaves, bring to a boil, and simmer, uncovered, for 2 minutes.

Purée in a blender or food processor or in the pan with an immersion blender until absolutely smooth. Return the purée to the rinsed pan and bring slowly to a simmer, then stir in the milk, remove from the heat, and set aside, covered, until cool enough to refrigerate. Pour into a large bowl or jug, cover with plastic wrap, and chill for at least 12 hours.

To serve, stir in the reserved watercress leaves and the sour cream or yogurt, taste, and add extra salt, if necessary. Garnish each serving with a scattering of pine nuts or sliced almonds.

HUNGARIAN CHERRY SOUP

SERVES 4
KEEPS FOR 3 DAYS IN THE FRIDGE
FREEZES WITHOUT THE CREAM FOR 3 MONTHS

Fruit soup can be made with a combination of fruits, including peaches, plums, cherries, or nectarines. It is then slightly thickened and enriched with smetana, or East European sour cream. The finest variety of fruit soup, however, is Yayin Duvdivanim. Made with morello cherries, it is known in its birth place, Budapest, as Hideg Meggyleves. Serve the soup as you would borscht (see page 42) as an appetizer in a glass. The flavor is best if the soup is prepared one day ahead.

1 lb/480g jar pitted Morello cherries in syrup (reserve a few for garnish)

²/₃ cup/150ml Port or red Kiddush wine

½ cup/4oz/125g sugar

grated zest of ½ lemon

½ tsp salt

1 cinnamon stick

1 tbsp cornstarch mixed to a cream with 1 tsp lemon juice and 1 tbsp water

scant 1 cup/200ml smetana or sour cream

Drain the cherries, reserving the syrup. Measure the syrup and add enough water to make 3 cups/750ml.

Put the syrup mixture, wine, sugar, lemon zest, salt, and cinnamon stick into a large pan, bring to a boil, and bubble, uncovered, for 7 minutes until the liquid is well flavored. Add the cherries and the cornstarch mixture, bring back to a boil, and simmer for 3 minutes until clear.

Cool until it stops steaming, then refrigerate until absolutely cold. Put the sour cream in a bowl and add a ladleful or two of the cold cherry mixture, whisking until smooth. Pour this creamy liquid back into the cherry mixture and chill until just before serving. Serve cold but not icy, garnished with a few of the reserved cherries.

CHILLED SUMMER FRUIT SOUP

SERVES 6–8

KEEPS FOR 3 DAYS IN THE FRIDGE | FREEZES FOR 3 MONTHS

German Jews who summered, before the Second World War, in cottages on the shores of the Baltic made marvelous cold soups from the fruits of high summer. The choice of ingredients depends on the season, but this combination of sweet and tart is particularly refreshing.

1 ¼ cups/8oz/225g fresh pitted plums

1 ¼ cups/8oz/225g pitted morello or other tart cherries

½ lb/225g peaches, sliced

1 pinch of salt

small cinnamon stick or 1 tsp ground cinnamon

⅓ cup/3oz/75g sugar

2 tbsp cornstarch

1 tbsp sweet red (Port-type) wine or water

⅔ cup/150ml sour cream

Put the fruit in a soup pot with 6¼ cups/1.5l water and add the salt, cinnamon, and sugar. Simmer, covered, for 15–20 minutes, or until the fruit is tender, then remove the cinnamon stick, if using, and force the mixture through a fine sieve, or purée in a blender (or in the pan with an immersion blender) until smooth.

Mix the cornstarch with the sweet red wine or water, stir into the soup, and simmer for 10 minutes until thickened and clear. Chill well.

Serve in soup cups, topped with sour cream, as a refreshing start to a summer meal.

POULTRY

OVEN-FRIED CHICKEN

SERVES 6
COOKED OR RAW CHICKEN FREEZES FOR 3 MONTHS

These crunchy portions of chicken are coated with a mixture of crumbs and herbs and are equally delicious hot or cold. They are cooked with only 5 tablespoons of oil, yet are as crisp as if they had been deep-fried. They make excellent "freezer-fillers" because they can be frozen either cooked or raw and ready to cook.

¼ cup/50ml lemon juice

6 bone-in chicken portions or boneless breasts, skin removed

FOR THE COATING

scant ½ cup/2oz/60g coating crumbs or medium matzo meal

1 egg

¼ cup/50ml sunflower oil

1 tsp salt

20 grinds of black pepper

3 tsp dried mixed herbs or herbes de Provence (optional)

1 tsp paprika

¼ tsp garlic salt (optional)

finely grated zest of 1 lemon

Put the lemon juice into a flat dish, turn the chicken pieces in it, then set aside for 1 hour. Turn once or twice.

Preheat the oven to 400°F/200°C. If you are using matzo meal or if the coating crumbs are pale in color, spread them out on a baking sheet and put them in the oven as it heats up, until they are golden brown (this gives a better color to the cooked chicken).

Whisk the egg and oil together with the salt and pepper until well blended and then put in a shallow dish large enough to hold a portion of chicken. Mix the coating crumbs, herbs, spices, and lemon zest in a dish of a similar size. Have ready a lightly greased oven tray large enough to hold the portions, well spaced, side by side. Lay each chicken piece in the egg mixture, using a pastry brush to coat it evenly, then roll it in the crumb mixture, again to coat evenly. Pat off any excess with your hands.

Arrange on the baking sheet and cook for 40 minutes (30 minutes for boneless breasts) until they are a rich brown color. There is no need to turn the chicken, since it will brown evenly on all sides. The chicken can be kept hot and crisp for up to 30 minutes in a warm oven at 200°F/100°C.

VARIATION
SESAME CHICKEN
Mix ½ cup/3oz/75g sesame seeds with the coating crumbs or meal.

BIBLICAL CHICKEN

SERVES 6

KEEPS FOR 2 DAYS IN THE FRIDGE | FREEZES FOR 2 MONTHS

I have discovered that for boneless chicken breasts, the briefer the cooking period, the better. So to produce a tender yet juicy breast, I fry it lightly on both sides and then, after deglazing the pan, simply leave to soak in the sauce for 1 or 2 hours. It then needs only bringing slowly back to simmering point in the sauce before serving.

6 skinless, partly boned chicken breasts, trimmed of rib-cage

1 ½ tbsp flour

1 tsp salt

10 grinds of black pepper

4 tbsp/2oz/50g margarine

1 tbsp sunflower or olive oil

½ cup/2oz/50g sliced almonds

1 cup/225ml dry white wine plus ½ cup/125ml homemade chicken stock (see page 176), or 1 ½ cups/ 350ml chicken stock made with a bouillon cube

½ cup/125ml orange juice

2 tsp grated lemon zest

1 tbsp clear honey

3 tbsp raisins, preferably muscatel (muscat)

3in/7.5cm cinnamon stick

2 tsp cornstarch mixed with 1 tbsp cold water or chicken stock

2 small oranges, peeled and cut into pith-free segments

basmati rice or baby potatoes, to serve

Take each breast in turn and flatten it gently between your hands. Season the flour with the salt and pepper, then coat the chicken with the seasoned flour. In a large sauté pan, heat the margarine and oil until the foam subsides, then immediately add the almonds and cook gently until golden brown. Drain on a paper towel, leaving the remaining oil in the pan.

Add the chicken breasts to the hot oil—probably in 2 batches if the pan is small—and cook on each side for about 3 minutes, or until golden. Remove from the pan and pour away any excess fat without discarding the savory brown bits at the bottom. If using, add the wine to the pan, stirring well, and bubble for 3 minutes to intensify the flavor, then add the stock, orange juice, lemon zest, honey, raisins, and cinnamon stick. Bring the sauce to a boil, add the chicken breasts in a single layer, spoon the liquid over them, then cover the pan and take it off the heat. Set aside for 1 to 2 hours.

Just before serving, bring the sauce slowly back to a simmer, add the cornstarch mixture, and bubble for 3 minutes. Pierce a breast to check that there's no sign of pinkness; if there is, bubble for 3 more minutes. Lift the breasts out and arrange them on a warm plate. Add salt and pepper if necessary, then spoon the sauce over the breasts and decorate the dish with the orange sections and the toasted almonds. Serve accompanied by basmati rice or baby potatoes.

POLLO EN PEPITORIA

SERVES 6
KEEPS FOR 2 DAYS IN THE FRIDGE | DO NOT FREEZE
BEST REHEATED IN THE MICROWAVE

This is a Spanish chicken dish that uses ground almonds to thicken the white wine sauce. The use of ground almonds as a thickener was common in medieval times, before the invention of a roux thickener. The chicken can be fried and the sauce prepared 1½ hours before serving.

scant ½ cup/2oz/50g flour

1 tsp salt

15 grinds of black pepper

6–8 skinless chicken breasts with wing attached

¼ cup/60ml olive oil

1 large onion, finely chopped

1 bay leaf

generous 1 cup/250ml dry white wine plus 1 cup/225ml homemade chicken stock (see page 176), or 2½ cups/500ml chicken stock made with a bouillon cube

½ cup/2oz/50g ground almonds

2 hard-boiled egg yolks

1 fat garlic clove, halved

¼ tsp turmeric or ground saffron

TO SERVE

¼ cup/1oz/25g sliced almonds, toasted in a dry pan

1 hard-boiled egg, grated and mixed with 1 tbsp chopped parsley

Put the flour, salt, and pepper into a plastic bag and shake the breasts in it, one at a time, until evenly coated. Heat the oil in a large sauté pan and fry the chicken breasts, a few at a time, until a rich golden brown. Drain on paper towels and transfer to a baking pan large enough to hold them in a single layer.

To make the sauce, sauté the onion in the same oil, covering the pan until a rich gold and beginning to "melt." Add the bay leaf and wine, if using, and bubble, uncovered, for 3 minutes to concentrate the flavor. Then add the stock, cover, and leave to simmer gently for 15 minutes.

Put the ground almonds, egg yolks, garlic, and turmeric or saffron in the bowl of a food processor. Process until pasty, then gradually add the simmering liquid, removing the bay leaf, and process until a smooth, creamy sauce is formed. Return to the saucepan, stir well, and leave covered until just before serving.

To complete the cooking, preheat the oven to 375°F/190°C and bake the chicken, uncovered, for 20 minutes until the juices run clear when the chicken is pierced with a sharp knife. Reheat the sauce gently until simmering. Arrange the chicken breasts on a heated platter and coat with the hot sauce. Scatter with the toasted almonds and the egg and parsley mixture.

CHICKEN IZMIR

SERVES 6

KEEPS FOR 2 DAYS IN THE FRIDGE | FREEZES FOR 3 MONTHS

This Turkish chicken dish with eggplant and warm spices is perfect for a spring dinner party. The sautéed eggplants give the sauce a distinctive rich, smooth flavor.

1 lb/450g eggplants, cut into ½in/1cm cubes

2 tbsp salt

½ cup/125ml sunflower oil

1 heaped tbsp flour

20 grinds of black pepper

6 chicken joints, skinned

1 tbsp olive oil

1 large onion, chopped

1 garlic clove, chopped

2½ cups/600ml vegetable stock

3 tbsp tomato paste

2 tsp brown sugar

½ tsp ground cinnamon

½ tsp ground cumin

½ tsp ground coriander

Preheat the oven to 325°F/160°C.

Place the eggplant cubes in a bowl, cover with cold water, and add 1 tablespoon of the salt. Leave for half an hour and then squeeze out as much moisture as possible, or use a salad spinner. Put the sunflower oil in a large frying pan and heat for 3 minutes. Add the eggplant, cover, and sauté on all sides until golden brown. Lift out and drain on paper towel.

Combine the flour with ½ teaspoon salt and 10 grinds of pepper. Dry the chicken pieces well and coat with the seasoned flour. In a Dutch oven or oven-to-table lidded sauté pan, fry the portions in the hot olive oil until they are a rich brown on all sides, then lift out and drain on paper towels to remove any surface fat.

In the same oil, gently sauté the chopped onion and garlic until they turn a rich brown. Keep the lid on for 5 minutes to soften them in the steam, then remove it to finish the browning.

Add the stock, tomato paste, 1 teaspoon salt, 10 grinds of black pepper, and the spices. Stir well to release any tasty crispy bits adhering to the base of the pot, then lay the chicken on top and surround with the fried eggplants. Bring to simmering point. Immediately cover and transfer to the oven. Bake for 50 minutes until the chicken is cooked through and the sauce is rich and thick.

SIRKE PAPRIKASH

SERVES 4

KEEPS FOR 3 DAYS IN THE FRIDGE | FREEZES FOR 2 MONTHS

This chicken paprika dish is the true Hungarian recipe. The quality of the paprika is the deciding factor in this simple but wonderfully flavorsome recipe, so buy the best quality you can find, ideally from a specialist spice shop. Kulonleges paprika, from Hungary, is the finest in quality and also the most finely ground.

3½lb/1.5kg chicken, backbone removed and cut into 4 portions on the bone, lightly salted

2 tbsp sunflower oil

1 onion, finely chopped

2 tbsp Hungarian paprika, preferably Kulonleges

⅔ cup/150ml chicken stock

2 green or red peppers, deseeded and cut into fine ¼in/5mm strips

14oz/400g canned chopped tomatoes

1 tsp cornstarch mixed until creamy with 3 tbsp cold water

1 tsp salt

10 grinds of black pepper

Dry the chicken pieces with paper towels, then heat the oil and sauté until golden. Remove. In the same oil, gently cook the onion, covered, for 10–15 minutes until softened and golden.

Stir in the paprika and chicken stock and cook for a further 2 minutes. Add the chicken with any juices, the pepper strips, and the tomatoes. Cover and cook very gently for 25–30 minutes until the chicken is cooked through—there will be no sign of pinkness when a piece is pierced with a sharp knife.

Lift the chicken pieces on to a warm platter. Add the cornstarch mixture to the sauté pan. Simmer for 3 minutes, stirring, or until thickened to a coating consistency. Add the salt and pepper, taste, and adjust the seasoning if necessary. Spoon the sauce over the chicken and serve.

KHORESH PORTAGAL
SWEET AND SOUR PERSIAN CHICKEN

SERVES 6
KEEPS FOR 2 DAYS IN THE FRIDGE | DO NOT FREEZE

Gently does it when cooking this exquisite chicken dish in a fruited sauce. The dish is adapted from medieval Persian cuisine. Cubes of chicken breast are simmered in a lightly spiced orange sauce on the lowest possible heat until they are meltingly tender. Serve the khoresh with the wonderful Persian chello rice (see page 170). It is equally delicious served at room temperature.

1/4 cup/60ml olive or sunflower oil

1 1/2–2 1/4lb/680g–1kg boneless, skinless chicken breast, patted dry and cut into 1in/2.5cm cubes

1 1/2 tsp paprika

1 1/2 tsp ground cinnamon

1/4 tsp freshly grated nutmeg

1/2 tsp salt

8 grinds of black pepper

about 1 1/4 cups/275ml chicken stock (see page 176)

1 large onion, finely sliced

2 tbsp/1oz/25g margarine

1 tsp sunflower oil

3 very large or 5 medium oranges, peeled and cut into pith-free segments

1/3 cup/3oz/75g granulated sugar

1/3 cup/75ml white wine vinegar or cider vinegar

1 1/2 tsp cornstarch mixed to a cream with 1 tbsp water, if needed

Heat the oil and fry the chicken over medium heat in a lidded sauté pan to seal it—it will turn white on all sides. Sprinkle on the spices and seasonings, mix well, cook a further 2 minutes, and then add enough stock to barely cover the chicken. Cover and cook on the lowest possible heat—with the stock just bubbling—until tender and white all the way through, about 10 minutes.

Meanwhile, slowly sauté the onion in the margarine and oil until it turns a rich, deep gold—don't over-brown, since this will impair the flavor. Put the oranges in another small saucepan, sprinkle with the sugar and vinegar, and cook gently, uncovered, for 15 minutes or until the fruit is sitting in a thick syrup.

Arrange the onion and its juices on top of the chicken, followed by the oranges and their syrup. Reheat very gently, covered, for 10 minutes. If the sauce seems thin, stir in the cornstarch mixture and simmer, stirring, for a further 3 minutes until clear.

SPICED CHICKEN PILAF

SERVES 6

LEFTOVERS KEEP FOR 2 DAYS IN THE FRIDGE | FREEZE FOR 3 MONTHS

Really fresh and fragrant spices and a well-flavored stock are essential ingredients that can transform a mundane Monday dish such as pilaf into a party sparkler. In this version, a blend of wild and long-grain rice, available in ready-mixed packages, adds extra texture. The elements of this richly satisfying dish can be cooked ahead and assembled just before serving.

3½lb/1.5kg chicken, quartered

1 onion

1 tsp salt

10 grinds of black pepper

large sprig parsley

1¼ cups/9oz/250g mixed long-grain and wild rice

1 bay leaf

2½ tbsp virgin olive oil

½ cup/2oz/50g sliced almonds, toasted in a dry pan

½ tsp sea salt

fresh cilantro leaves or flat-leaf parsley, chopped

FOR THE SAUCE

1 cup/225ml homemade chicken stock (see page 176)

1 tsp ground cumin

2 tsp freshly ground coriander seeds

1 tsp freshly grated ginger

1 garlic clove, crushed with a little sea salt

16 grinds of black pepper

To cook the bird, put it in a pan with 2½ cups/575ml water and the onion, salt, pepper, and parsley. Cover with foil and then a lid to keep in the steam and simmer very gently for 1 hour until absolutely tender.

Lift out the chicken, remove the skin and bones, and cut the meat into bite-sized strips. Boil the stock, if necessary, down to 2½ cups/575ml, then strain through a sieve and reserve.

To cook the rice, place it in a heavy-based saucepan with the bay leaf and reserved stock, cover, and bring to a boil over moderate heat. Stir well, reduce the heat, and simmer for 20 minutes, or until the liquid has been absorbed and the rice is cooked but still has bite to it. Discard the bay leaf. Set aside.

To make the sauce put the homemade stock in a small saucepan over a moderate heat and stir in the cumin, coriander, ginger, garlic, and pepper. Simmer for 5 minutes, remove from the heat, and set aside.

Just before serving, heat the olive oil in a large frying pan and tip in the cooked rice, toasted nuts, and sea salt with enough of the reheated sauce to moisten. Turn the mixture around in the oil until heated through. Meanwhile, gently reheat the chicken either on the stove, in a steamer lined with oiled foil, or covered in the microwave for 2–3 minutes. Arrange the chicken and rice on a large warmed serving dish, moisten with the sauce, and scatter over the cilantro or parsley. Serve, passing around any extra sauce separately.

MOROCCAN CHICKEN PILAF
WITH FRUIT AND NUTS

SERVES 6

KEEPS FOR 3 DAYS IN THE FRIDGE | FREEZES FOR 3 MONTHS

This pilaf can be cooked well ahead, then reheated in a moderate oven or the microwave, but the chicken does need to be stir-fried just before serving—it toughens when reheated.

heaped ½ cup/4½oz/125g mixed wild and brown rice

1¼ cups/8oz/225g white basmati rice

2½ tbsp salt

3½ tbsp sunflower or vegetable oil

1 bunch of scallion bulbs, finely chopped

⅔ cup/4oz/100g dried apricots, chopped with kitchen scissors

⅔ cup/2oz/50g shelled pistachios

½ cup/2oz/50g pine nuts

2 tbsp ground cinnamon

1 tsp ground cumin

15 grinds of black pepper, plus more to taste

1 lb 2oz/500g boneless, skinless chicken breast, cut into strips about 3 x ½in/7.5 x 1cm

3 tbsp lemon juice

To cook the rice, combine the varieties, cover with cold water, and soak for 30 minutes. Strain and rinse thoroughly under the faucet until the water runs clear. Bring a large heavy saucepan of water to a boil with 2 tablespoons of the salt. Add the rice and cook, uncovered, bubbling steadily for 7 minutes, or until a grain feels almost tender when bitten. Turn into a strainer and rinse thoroughly under hot running water, then drain well. Coat the bottom of the pan with 1 tablespoon of the oil, then add the rice. Wrap a dish towel under the lid of the pan, then place it firmly into position so that you have a perfect seal. Steam over the lowest possible heat for 20 minutes.

Meanwhile, put 1 tablespoon oil into a medium sauté pan and cook the onions briskly until golden, then add the apricots, pistachios, and pine nuts, sprinkling them with 1½ tablespoons cinnamon and the cumin as they cook. Using a slotted spoon, remove this mixture from the pan and stir it into the cooked rice, together with 1 teaspoon salt and the pepper. Transfer to a microwave-safe dish. Season the chicken and sprinkle with the lemon juice. Set aside.

Just before serving, reheat the rice in the microwave, covered, on 100 percent power for 2–3 minutes, then stir gently with a fork.

Meanwhile, heat the remaining 1½ tablespoons of oil and stir-fry the chicken strips for 3 minutes, sprinkling them with the remaining cinnamon, then stir into the reheated rice. Serve on a shallow platter.

ROAST CHICKEN WITH PINE NUTS

SERVES 6
KEEPS FOR 3 DAYS IN THE FRIDGE | FREEZES FOR 3 MONTHS

Strewing the breast of the bird with fresh herbs and adding pine nuts to the gravy transforms plain roast chicken into something extra special.

5–5½lb/2–2.25kg roasting chicken

3 tbsp fresh lemon juice

1 eating apple, quartered

olive oil

sea salt

10 grinds of black pepper

12 shallots, peeled

3 tbsp chopped mixed herbs

¼ cup/1 oz/25g pine nuts

½ cup/125ml each dry white wine and chicken stock, or 1 cup/225ml stock alone

2 tsp cornstarch mixed until creamy with 3 tbsp cold water

1 pinch of sugar (optional)

1 small bunch of parsley

Preheat the oven to 375°F/190°C. Pat the cavity of the bird dry, squeeze the lemon juice into it, insert the apple, and carefully place the bird onto a rack standing in a roasting pan, breast-side down. Brush lightly with olive oil and sprinkle with ground sea salt and the pepper.

Roast for 1 hour 20 minutes, basting every 20 minutes. Turn the bird over, breast-side up, and slip the shallots underneath the rack. Brush the breast lightly with olive oil, season again, and strew with the chopped herbs. Roast for a further 40 minutes, basting once, until the chicken is a rich golden brown and the juices run clear when the leg is pierced with a skewer.

Meanwhile, sauté the pine nuts gently in a little oil until golden brown. Lift the bird on to a carving dish and set aside in a warm place. Remove the shallots with a slotted spoon and keep hot. Put the roasting pan on top of the stove and drain off the fat from the dish. Add the pine nuts, wine, and stock with the cornstarch mixture. Bubble for 3 minutes, stirring, taste, and re-season if necessary. (Add a pinch of sugar if too acidic.) Stir in the parsley.

Portion or carve the bird and serve with the pine nuts and sauce. The golden-brown shallots can be served alongside.

ROAST TURKEY WITH A FRUITED BULGAR STUFFING

SERVES 4–6

LEFTOVERS KEEP FOR 3 DAYS IN THE FRIDGE | FREEZE FOR 3 MONTHS

4½–5½lb/2–2.5kg turkey

FOR THE STUFFING

scant ½ cup/2oz/60g dried apricots

scant ½ cup/2oz/60g dried pears

about 1½ cups/350ml boiling water

2 tbsp olive oil

1 onion, chopped

1 large garlic clove, chopped

1 tbsp finely chopped fresh ginger

1 cup/6oz/175g bulgar

3 cups/700ml hot chicken stock

¼ cup/1oz/25g pine nuts, lightly toasted in a dry pan

½ tsp freshly grated nutmeg

finely grated zest of 2 lemons

1 tsp salt

10 grinds of black pepper

FOR THE GLAZE

2 tbsp clear honey

2 tbsp fresh lemon juice

First prepare the stuffing. Cover the dried fruit with boiling water and leave to plump up for 30 minutes, then coarsely chop. Next, heat 1 tablespoon of the olive oil in a lidded sauté pan and cook the onion and garlic for 5 minutes until a rich gold color. Stir in the ginger and cook for a further minute, then add the bulgar, coating it well with the oil. Add 5 cups/1.2l of the stock and the dried fruit, cover, and cook over very low heat for about 10 minutes, or until the liquid has been absorbed. Stir in the pine nuts, nutmeg, lemon zest, salt, and pepper. Set aside.

Preheat the oven to 450°F/230°C. Fill the cavity of the bird loosely with some of the stuffing, then tie the legs together to make it a compact shape. Oil a roasting pan and set a rack in it, then arrange the bird on top and brush all over with the remaining oil. Put the remaining stuffing in an oven-proof dish, cover tightly, and set aside. Put the bird in the oven, then turn the temperature down to 375°F/190°C. Roast the bird, allowing 20 minutes for each 1lb/450g, based on its weight before stuffing.

While the bird is roasting, mix together the honey and lemon juice. Thirty minutes before the bird is done, brush all over with a third of the glaze, and put the dish with the bulgar in the oven to cook. After a further 15 minutes, brush again with the glaze, and brush again when the bird is cooked. Transfer a warm dish to rest.

Meanwhile, pour the remaining stock into the roasting pan and stir well over moderate heat, then pour the liquid through a sieve into a saucepan. Skim off as much fat as possible, then boil down until it is smooth and well seasoned. Serve hot with the sliced bird and the stuffing.

HEN CASSEROLE
HAIMISCHE STYLE

SERVES 4–6, DEPENDING ON THE SIZE OF THE BIRD
LEFTOVERS KEEP FOR 3 DAYS IN THE FRIDGE | FREEZE FOR 3 MONTHS

Fowls (or stewing hens) are specially bred for the Jewish market and are available from most kosher butchers. They are about 12 months old, firm-fleshed, and mature enough to make excellent soup, yet still young enough to be tender and flavorsome in stews. A fine plump fowl has, perhaps, more flavor than any other kind of bird. This is the ultimate comfort-food casserole.

1 tsp salt

10 grinds of black pepper

2 tsp flour

2 tsp paprika

1 fowl (stewing hen),
4½–5½lb/2–2.25kg,
made kosher and scalded

1 tbsp oil

1 large onion, thinly sliced

1 garlic clove, crushed

1 bay leaf

1 carrot, thinly sliced

2 soft tomatoes, or
2½ tbsp tomato paste

½ cup/125ml homemade chicken stock (see page 176) or traditional chicken soup (see page 34)

ANY OR ALL OF THE FOLLOWING VEGETABLES:

½ red or yellow pepper, deseeded and cut into strips

3 celery stalks, sliced

1¼ cups/4oz/125g mushrooms, sliced

Preheat the oven to 350°F/180°C. Mix the salt, pepper, flour, and paprika, then rub into the bird's skin.

In a heavy Dutch oven, heat the oil and fry the onion and garlic until soft and golden, then add the bay leaf, carrot, tomatoes or paste, and your chosen vegetables, and stir over gentle heat until they have absorbed most of the oil. Put the bird in and turn it in the hot oil until it turns pale gold. Pour the stock or soup down the side of the casserole dish. Cover and transfer to the oven.

After 15 minutes, turn the oven down to 325°F/160°C and cook for 3 hours, or until the bird is a rich golden brown and the leg can be moved easily in its socket. During cooking, the liquid should be bubbling very gently. If the bubbling is too violent, turn the oven down to 300°F/150°C. Baste twice with the pan juices.

To serve, lift the bird onto a warm platter. Skim off as much fat as possible. Remove the bay leaf, then blend or process the vegetables and liquid until absolutely smooth—this produces a marvelous naturally thickened gravy. Bring to a boil, taste, and re-season if necessary, then serve.

DUCK BREASTS WITH A HONEY AND GINGER GLAZE

SERVES 6
LEFTOVERS KEEP FOR 3 DAYS IN THE FRIDGE | FREEZE FOR 2 MONTHS

This recipe produces a duck in the Chinese style with a mahogany brown, crunchy skin. No sauce is necessary, but a fruity salad of chicory and orange makes a refreshing accompaniment.

6 large duck breasts, on the bone

2 rounded tbsp peeled and finely chopped young ginger root

freshly ground black pepper

juice of 1 small orange

2½ tbsp clear honey

2 tsp soy sauce

1 pinch of salt

a salad of orange segments, chicory, and a sprinkling of sesame seeds, to serve (optional)

Remove any lumps of fat from the duck joints and prick all over, piercing only the skin, not the flesh.

Lay the duck pieces side by side in a large dish, scatter with the ginger, and sprinkle with the black pepper, rubbing in well. Pour in the orange juice, then turn the duck pieces to make sure they are evenly moistened on all sides. Cover and set aside for several hours in a cool place, or overnight in the fridge.

To cook the duck breasts, preheat the oven to 400°F/200°C. Drain the marinade from the duck and scrape off the ginger, then mix them together and reserve.

Arrange the breasts on a rack in a roasting pan and roast for 15 minutes. Mix the honey with the reserved marinade and stir in the soy sauce and salt to make a glaze.

Pour off all the fat that has collected under the duck, then paint the portions all over with the glaze. Roast for another 10 minutes, basting once. At the end of this time the duck should be a mahogany brown and deliciously tender. If it seems to be browning too quickly, cover loosely with a tent of foil.

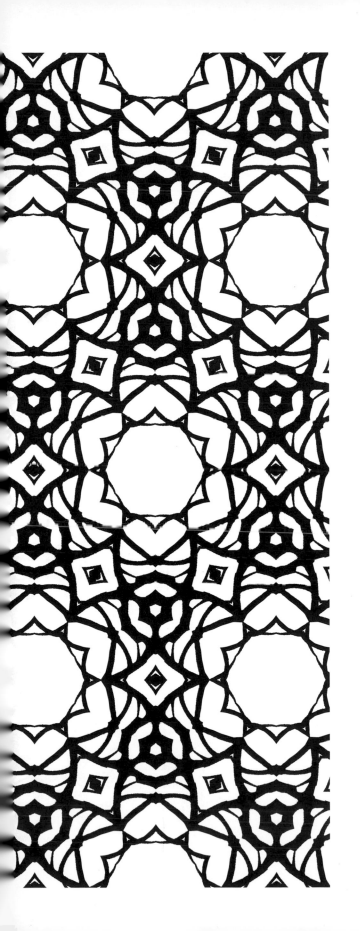

MEAT

CHOLENT

SERVES 6

KEEPS FOR 3 DAYS IN THE FRIDGE | LEFTOVERS FREEZE FOR 3 MONTHS

This dish goes by several names—cholent, sholent, or shalet to name a few—and the ingredients, though basically meat, potatoes, and fat, vary according to the whim and location of the cook. But, as one Jewish food writer puts it, this ancient Sabbath recipe is best defined as "any dish that has the stamina to stand up to 24 hours in the oven."

2½ cups/1 lb/450g dried butter beans (or lima beans), soaked overnight

4lb/1.75kg piece of boneless brisket point

½ tsp salt

20 grinds of pepper

1 tsp paprika

1 tsp ground ginger

2 tbsp chicken fat or margarine

3 onions, sliced

1 garlic clove, crushed

1 bay leaf

6 peeled whole potatoes or 1¼ cups/8oz/225g pearl barley

Drain the beans well. Preheat the oven to 400°F/200°C.

Rub the brisket with the salt, pepper, paprika, and ginger, then brown quickly in the chicken fat or margarine, together with the onions and garlic. Put in a deep earthenware hot-pot or Dutch oven. Add the bay leaf, beans, and the potatoes or barley.

Cover with boiling water, put a lid on the dish, and place in the oven for 30 minutes, or until the contents start to bubble. Turn the heat right down to 225°F/110°C, and allow to cook overnight. Serve for lunch the next day.

VARIATION
If you would like to serve the dish as an accompaniment rather than a main course, use only 1¼ cups/8oz/225g beans, ½lb/225g beef, and a knuckle bone, if available, for flavor.

BRAISED BRISKET POT ROAST

SERVES 4–6, PLUS LEFTOVERS FOR SANDWICHES
COOKED MEAT KEEPS FOR 3 DAYS IN THE FRIDGE | FREEZES FOR 3 MONTHS

One of the tastiest of kosher cuts. Leftover brisket should be forced into a bowl, covered with a saucer and a 2¼lb/1kg weight, and then refrigerated. The next day it will cut to perfection.

3lb/1.5kg brisket point

1 tbsp sunflower or olive oil

1 bay leaf

6 peppercorns

2 tsp salt

10 grinds of black pepper

6 pearl onions or shallots, peeled

¾ cup/185ml boiling water

2 large potatoes, thickly sliced

2 carrots, thickly sliced

Preheat the oven to 300°F/150°C.

Brown the meat quickly in the hot oil. Sprinkle with the seasonings. Put in a casserole dish surrounded with the onions or shallots and the boiling water. Cover and cook in the oven for 3 hours.

An hour before the meat is ready, surround it with the potato and carrot slices. Serve the brisket cut into thick slices, together with the potatoes and carrots, in the delicious meat juices.

TSIMMES

**SERVES 6 AS A MAIN COURSE, 8 AS A SIDE DISH—BUT YOU CAN NEVER
MAKE ENOUGH TSIMMES TO SATISFY EVERYONE**

A tsimmes—a sweet carrot and brisket casserole—might be called a Jewish hotpot, for its flavor depends on long, slow cooking, during which the sweet elements in it—be they carrots, dried fruits, sweet potatoes, squash, honey, or syrup—slowly caramelize, giving rise to a glorious aroma.

2lb/900g slice of brisket, excess fat trimmed, and cut into 1½in/4cm chunks

3½lb/1.5kg carrots, peeled and cut into ½in/1.25cm cubes

¼ cup/60ml honey or golden syrup, or more to taste

½ tsp white pepper

2 tsp salt

1 tbsp cornstarch mixed until creamy with 2 tbsp water

1½lb/680g potatoes, peeled and cut into large cubes

FOR THE DUMPLING (OPTIONAL)

6 tbsp/3oz/75g butter or margarine

scant 1½ cups/6oz/175g self-rising flour

½ tsp salt

Put the meat and carrots into a pan, barely cover with hot water, add 2 tablespoons of the honey or syrup, the pepper and ½ teaspoon of the salt, bring to a boil, and simmer for 2 hours either on top of the stove or in a slow oven. Skim the fat, or, if possible, chill overnight so that most of the fat can be removed.

Four hours before you want to serve the tsimmes, make the dumpling by rubbing the margarine into the flour and salt. Gradually add about 5–6 tablespoons water (more, if needed) and mix to a dough. Put the dumpling in the middle of a large oval Dutch oven. Lift the meat and carrots from their cooking liquid with a slotted spoon and arrange around the dumpling.

Preheat the oven to 300°F/150°C. Stir the cornstarch mixture into the cooking stock. Bring to a boil, stirring, then pour over the carrots and meat. Arrange the potatoes on top, adding extra boiling water if necessary so that they are just submerged. Sprinkle with the remaining salt and honey or syrup. Cover and bring to a boil on the stovetop (taking care that the bottom of the dumpling does not burn), then transfer to the oven and cook for 3½ hours.

Uncover and taste, adding a little more syrup or honey if necessary. Allow to brown for a further half an hour, then serve.

STUFATO DI MANZO FIORENTINA

FLORENTINE BEEF STEW WITH RED WINE AND ROSEMARY

SERVES 4-6
KEEPS FOR 3 DAYS IN THE FRIDGE | FREEZES FOR 3 MONTHS

3 tbsp olive oil

2 garlic cloves, finely chopped

1 tsp fresh or dried rosemary, finely chopped or crumbled

2½lb/1.25kg flavorful stewing beef, cut into 1in/2.5cm chunks

1 tsp salt

10 grinds of black pepper

2 tsp brown sugar

1 cup/250ml dry red wine

²/₃ cup/150ml beef stock

¼ cup/60ml tomato paste

1 tsp dried Italian seasoning herbs

1 tbsp chopped parsley

1 tbsp chopped basil

TO SERVE

12oz/350g dry penne or fusilli pasta, cooked according to the package directions

Heat the oil in a saucepan and gently sauté the garlic and rosemary to flavor it. Dry the meat well with paper towels. Sauté the well-dried meat in the flavored oil until it is richly browned all over, and sprinkle it with the salt, pepper, and sugar. Don't crowd the pan—if necessary, fry the meat in 2 batches.

Pour in the wine and bubble fiercely for 3 minutes to concentrate the flavor, then add the stock, tomato paste, and dried herbs. Cover and simmer for 2 hours on the stovetop, or 2½ hours in an oven preheated to 300°F/150°C. The meat should be bathed in a thick sauce. Stir in the parsley and basil. Serve with the cooked pasta.

PAN-SEARED KOSHER RIB-EYE STEAK

SERVES 4

Kosher steaks are best when seared on the stove, either in a heavy-based frying pan or preferably in a ridged stove-top cast-iron grill pan. To ensure tenderness, ask your butcher to cut the steaks from a side of beef that has been hung for 7–10 days. To ensure perfectly cooked steak, use an instant-read meat thermometer. The temperature continues to rise as the meat rests, so remove it from the heat when it reaches 5 degrees below your target temperature (for example, 130°F/55°C for medium-rare).

4 rib-eye steaks, each 6–8oz/175–225g and ¾–1 in/2–2.5cm thick

black pepper, to taste

sunflower or vegetable oil

FOR THE SAUCE

⅔ cup/150ml dry white or red wine, white vermouth, leftover gravy, or good-quality stock

2 tsp dark soy sauce

1 tsp sea salt

a few grinds of black pepper

1 tbsp chopped parsley

Remove the steaks from the fridge 1 hour before cooking. Trim most of the fat from each steak, leaving only a very thin edging. Dry well with paper towels. Sprinkle with freshly ground black pepper.

Heat the pan over high heat until a sprinkling of water sizzles and evaporates as soon as it hits the surface (it should be extremely hot). Brush very lightly with oil using a piece of paper towel, then put in the steaks. Sear the meat for 3–4 minutes, then turn and cook on the other side for a further 4–6 minutes, turning the steaks again if necessary. Check the temperature with a meat thermometer, or pierce one steak and, if it's the right color in the center, immediately transfer to a warm plate and leave to rest while you make the sauce.

Turn down the heat and add the wine, vermouth, gravy, or stock to the pan. Swirl this around to loosen the delicious sediment sticking to the bottom; if using a ridged pan, you may find a small silicone brush helpful for this. Allow to simmer for a minute or so until slightly reduced to concentrate the flavor. Add the soy sauce, salt, pepper, and parsley, then pour over the steak and serve immediately.

ALBONDIGAS AL BUYOR
GREEK–JEWISH MEATBALLS IN A SWEET-AND-SOUR SAUCE

SERVES 4
KEEPS FOR 4 DAYS IN THE FRIDGE | FREEZES FOR 3 MONTHS

FOR THE MEATBALLS

2 large eggs

1 slice white or brown bread, 1in/2.5cm thick, torn into pieces

½ small onion, quartered

½ tsp salt

7 grinds of black pepper

1½ tsp dark soy sauce

1 large sprig of parsley

1½ lb/500g ground beef

1 tbsp flour mixed with a pinch of salt and pepper

3 tbsp sunflower or vegetable oil

FOR THE SAUCE

1 onion, finely chopped

2 tsp salt

10 grinds of black pepper

3 tbsp brown sugar or 2 tbsp clear honey

2 tsp Dijon or English mustard

2 tsp soy sauce

1 tbsp lemon juice

½ cup/5oz/150g tomato paste, diluted with 1 cup/225ml water

For the meatballs, mix the eggs, torn bread, onion, salt, pepper, soy sauce, and parsley in a food processor for 30 seconds, or until smooth. Transfer the egg mixture to a bowl and mix in the raw meat with your hands or a large fork until smoothly blended. Set aside for 30 minutes. With wet hands, shape the mixture into patties or balls.

Put the seasoned flour on a piece of parchment paper, and dip each ball into it. Shake off any excess flour.

Heat the oil in a heavy frying pan for 4 minutes, put in the meatballs, and fry steadily until they are a rich brown color on both sides (you may need to do this in batches). Transfer to a plate using a slotted spoon, leaving behind any oil in the pan.

Now make the sauce. In the same pan, sauté the onion until golden. Add all the remaining sauce ingredients and simmer for 5 minutes.

Place the meatballs in a casserole dish or Dutch oven, pour in the sauce, and cover. Either simmer on the stovetop for 30 minutes or bake in a slow oven at 300°F/150°C for 45 minutes.

GEFILTE PAPRIKA-STUFFED PEPPERS, HUNGARIAN STYLE

SERVES 4–6
KEEPS FOR 3 DAYS IN THE FRIDGE | FREEZES FOR 2 MONTHS

This recipe is a more sophisticated version than often found—note the wine in the sauce, reflecting the cuisine soignée ("cooking with care"), typical of this part of Europe. This dish can be cooked on the stovetop, in the oven, or even in the microwave.

FOR THE SAUCE

1 onion, chopped

1 tbsp oil

½ cup/5oz/150g tomato paste

1¼ cups/275ml hot water

3 tbsp demerara sugar

3 tbsp lemon juice

½ tsp pumpkin pie spice or ground cinnamon

⅔ cup/150ml white wine (optional but nice) or water

FOR THE PEPPERS AND STUFFING

4–6 squat red bell peppers

1 egg, beaten

1 onion, grated

1 tsp salt

½ tsp mustard

1 tsp paprika

1 lb/450g lean ground beef

2 tsp matzo meal or oatmeal

If the peppers are to be stewed on top of the stove, use the same deep pan to make the sauce. Fry the onion in the oil until soft and golden. Add all the remaining sauce ingredients. Simmer, uncovered, for 20 minutes.

Slice off and retain the tops of the peppers and remove the seeds and ribs. Place the pepper shells in a saucepan and pour boiling water over them, then leave for 5 minutes. In a large bowl, mix the egg, onion salt, mustard, and paprika. Then mix in the meat and matzo meal or oatmeal. Drain the peppers on paper towel, then stuff with the meat mixture and cover each pepper with its top. Arrange them in the pan in which the sauce is simmering. Cover with foil, and then with the lid of the pan. Simmer gently for 1 hour, basting twice. When done, the sauce will be thick and the peppers tender.

Alternatively, transfer the sauce and stuffed peppers to a deep lidded casserole dish and cook in the oven at 325°F/170°C for 1½ hours.

To cook in the microwave, mix the sauce ingredients in a jug and cook uncovered on 100 percent (1000W) power for 3 minutes or until bubbling. Arrange the stuffed peppers side by side in a 12½ cup/3l deep, lidded casserole dish. Pour the sauce around them and cook on the highest setting for 6 minutes, or until bubbling, then reduce to 40 percent power and cook for a further 15 minutes or until the peppers feel tender when pierced with a sharp knife. Let it stand for 5 minutes before serving.

SEPHARDI-STYLE PIZZA

SERVES 6 | MAKES 2 X 10IN/25CM PIZZAS
OVEN-READY PIZZA FREEZES FOR 3 MONTHS

Middle Eastern Jews have been making this very special version of pizza for centuries. It is made, of course, without cheese and is topped instead with cumin-scented ground beef. Defrost frozen pizzas at room temperature for 2 hours, then bake as though freshly prepared.

FOR THE PIZZA DOUGH

2 tsp/¼oz/7g instant yeast or ¼ cake/½oz/14g fresh yeast

scant 3 cups/11oz/300g all-purpose flour

1½ tsp salt

1½ tsp sugar

3 tbsp olive oil

1 egg

⅔ cup/150ml hand-hot water

FOR THE TOPPING

1 onion, finely chopped

2 tbsp olive oil

1 lb/450g lean ground beef

1 tbsp tomato paste

1 tsp brown sugar

1 tsp salt

10 grinds of black pepper

1 tsp ground allspice

1 tsp ground cumin

1 good pinch of Cayenne pepper or chili flakes

3 tbsp chopped parsley

1 tbsp lemon juice

4½oz/125g frying wurst (kosher beef salami)

If using instant yeast, mix it with the flour, salt, and sugar; if using fresh yeast, dissolve it in the water. Mix all the ingredients together to form a soft but nonsticky ball of dough (add some extra flour if necessary); knead by hand or machine until smooth.

Put the dough in an oiled mixing bowl, turn it over so that it is coated with the oil, then cover with plastic wrap and leave in the kitchen until it has doubled in bulk—about 1 hour.

To make the topping, cook the finely chopped onions in the oil, covered, until softened and golden, then mix in a bowl with all the remaining ingredients except the wurst, using your hands to make sure the mixture is evenly blended together.

Preheat the oven to 450°F/230°C. Grease two baking sheets or 10in/25cm pizza pans. Divide the risen dough in half, knead each portion for 1–2 minutes to evenly distribute the gas bubbles, then roll or press out into two 10in/25cm rounds and place on the baking sheets or in the pizza pans.

Spread each round with an even layer of the topping, making sure the dough is covered right to the edges, then decorate with finely sliced wurst. Bake for 15 minutes until the meat is a rich brown and the wurst has curled. Serve at once.

PASTELES

MAKES ABOUT 16 SMALL PIES
BAKED OR UNBAKED PASTELES FREEZE FOR 2 MONTHS

The filling of these Sephardi meat pies is seasoned with allspice and contains fried pine nuts, which give them a satisfying texture.

FOR THE MEAT FILLING

2 tbsp/1oz/25g pine nuts

1 tbsp sunflower oil

1 onion, finely chopped

1lb/450g ground beef or lamb

1/2 cup/100ml cold water

1/2 tsp ground cinnamon

1/2 tsp ground allspice

1 tsp salt

10 grinds of black pepper

FOR THE PASTRY

2 3/4 cups/12oz/350g
all-purpose flour, plus extra for
dusting

1 tsp salt

3/4 cup/6oz/175g baking margarine,
cut into chunks

2 tbsp sunflower oil

4–5 tbsp warm water

FOR THE TOPPING

1 egg, beaten

sesame seeds

Fry the pine nuts gently in the oil until brown, then drain. Put the chopped onion into the pan and brown gently, add the meat, and continue to cook until it is brown all over. Barely cover with the water, add the spices, and simmer, uncovered, until the moisture has almost evaporated and the meat looks juicy. Stir in the pine nuts.

To make the pastry and shape the pasteles, put the flour, salt, and margarine in a large bowl. Sprinkle with the oil and mix together. Sprinkle with enough of the water to make a firm but nonsticky dough.

Preheat the oven to 400°F/200°C. Roll out the pastry 1/2in/2.5mm thick on a lightly floured board and, using metal pastry cutters, cut the dough into 16 rounds, 3 1/2–4in/8–9cm in diameter, and 16 rounds, 2in/5cm in diameter. Place the larger circles of pastry in muffin or patty pans, add a spoonful of cooled meat mixture, moisten the edges of the pastry, and top with the smaller round, sealing the edges.

Alternatively, to shape the pasteles in the traditional Sephardi way, use your fingers to pleat the edges of the larger circles to form cups 3/4in/2cm deep. Fill with the cooled meat, then moisten the edges, place a small circle on top, and press the two together with your thumbs to seal in the meat. Arrange on ungreased baking sheets about 1in/2.5cm apart.

Whichever way you shape them, brush the filled pies with beaten egg and scatter with sesame seeds. Bake for 20–25 minutes, or until a rich brown color.

LE GIGOT QUI PLEURE

SERVES 6

LEFTOVERS KEEP FOR 3 DAYS IN THE FRIDGE | FREEZE FOR 3 MONTHS

In this recipe for Kosher-style rolled shoulder of lamb, the aroma is intensified by spiking the meat with rosemary several hours before cooking. The exotic name comes from the meat juices dripping into the vegetables.

3lb/1.5kg boned and rolled lamb shoulder

2 sprigs fresh rosemary

2 garlic cloves, slivered

TO COAT THE LAMB

20 grinds of black pepper

olive oil

1 tsp mustard powder

1 tbsp flour

TO COOK BENEATH THE LAMB

1lb 10oz/750g baby potatoes, scrubbed

1 tsp salt

12oz/350g shallots

2½ cups/575ml meat stock (see page 176)

2 tbsp demerara or other raw sugar

FOR THE SAUCE

juices from the roasting pan

boiling water

1 tbsp cornstarch

⅓ cup plus 1 tbsp/90ml red wine

Several hours in advance, pierce the lamb at 2in/5cm intervals, and insert a tiny sprig of rosemary and a sliver of garlic in each incision.

Preheat the oven to 350°F/180°C. Sprinkle the lamb with pepper, brush with olive oil, and sprinkle with the mixed mustard and flour, then arrange on a rack that fits 2in/5cm above a roasting pan.

Put the potatoes into a saucepan of cold water, add the salt, and bring to a boil. Lift out with a slotted spoon and arrange the potatoes in the roasting pan. In the same water, bring the shallots to a boil, then quickly pour them into a strainer and drench with cold water. The skins can now be easily removed. Arrange the shallots with the potatoes in the roasting pan. Bring the stock to a boil, then pour over and around the potatoes and shallots. Lay the meat on its rack on top of the vegetables, put in the oven, and cook for 2¼ hours.

After 1 hour, take out the roasting pan and lift the meat on its rack so that you can stir the vegetables. Replace the meat, sprinkle with the sugar, and return to the oven. Check after half an hour, and if the stock seems to be drying up, add a little more hot water.

Transfer the meat to a dish and set aside, loosely covered with foil, or in the oven turned to its lowest setting. Lift out the vegetables with a slotted spoon and place on a serving dish. Cover and keep warm, but allow the meat to rest for 20 minutes before slicing and serving.

FOR THE SAUCE
Put the roasting pan on the stovetop and add enough boiling water to make the liquid up to 1¼ cups/275ml, then stir well to release all the delicious sediment. Mix the cornstarch to a creamy consistency with the wine and add it to the pan. Bubble for 3 minutes, stirring well, then taste and re-season if needed. (At this stage you may wish to transfer the sauce to a small saucepan to keep hot.)

ROAST STUFFED LAMB
WITH APRICOT OR MINT STUFFING

SERVES 6–8

LEFTOVERS KEEP FOR 3 DAYS IN THE FRIDGE | RAW STUFFING FREEZES FOR 1 MONTH

This recipe produces a particularly succulent joint that is equally delicious eaten cold the next day.

3¹/₂lb/1.5kg boneless lamb shoulder

APRICOT STUFFING

4 tbsp/2oz/60g margarine

1 small onion, finely chopped

scant 1 cup/4oz/125g unsulfured dried apricots, soaked overnight in cold water and drained, or partially rehydrated apricots, roughly chopped

grated zest of ¹/₂ lemon

¹/₂ tsp salt

1 pinch of white pepper

2 cups/4oz/125g fresh breadcrumbs

1 egg, beaten

MINT STUFFING

4 tbsp/2oz/60g margarine or oil

1 small onion, chopped

3 cups/6oz/175g fresh breadcrumbs

2 tsp each finely chopped mint and parsley

1 tsp salt

¹/₄ tsp black pepper

1 egg, beaten

Ask your butcher to bone the meat leaving a pocket for the stuffing, if possible. If this is not possible, the boned meat can be spread with the stuffing, then rolled before roasting.

To make either stuffing, melt the margarine or oil in a small frying pan and cook the onion gently until softened and golden. Put all the other ingredients into a bowl, except the egg, then mix in the onion and oil until well blended. Moisten with the beaten egg. The mixture should just cling together.

To stuff a pocketed shoulder, just pack the stuffing lightly into the pocket and sew it up into a firm, compact shape using a large needle and twine. To stuff and roll a shoulder, lay the meat, skin-side down, on a board and cut out any lumps of fat. Spread the stuffing evenly over the meat, pushing it into any little folds. Roll up neatly and sew into a compact shape, or skewer closed, if possible.

To roast the meat, preheat the oven to 350°F/180°C. Put a rack in a roasting pan and lay the meat on top. Sprinkle with the salt and pepper for the coating (overleaf), dust lightly with flour, then pour on the oil. Roast the meat for 2 hours, then sprinkle with the sugar and increase the heat to 400°F/200°C. Cook for a further 20–30 minutes until a rich brown color. Leave to rest in a warm place (or in the oven turned down to 225°F/110°C) for 15 minutes before carving.

Continued on page 83

FOR THE COATING

1 tsp salt

10 grinds of black pepper

dusting of flour

2 tbsp oil

1 tbsp demerara or other raw sugar

FOR THE GRAVY

1¼ cups/275ml water

2 tsp cornstarch

1 beef bouillon cube

For the gravy, pour off all but 2 teaspoons of fat from the roasting pan. Mix the cold water and cornstarch to a smooth consistency, then pour into the roasting pan and add the crumbled bouillon cube. Bring to a boil, stirring well, then season to taste with salt and pepper. Serve piping hot with the carved lamb.

HERBED LAMB CHOPS

SERVES 4

This is the basic method for grilling first-cut lamb chops, also known as cutlets or rib chops.

1 tbsp extra virgin olive oil

1 garlic clove, halved

1 tsp each of dried basil and rosemary or 1 tbsp each of the chopped fresh herbs

1 tbsp lemon juice

black pepper

8 first-cut lamb chops ¾in/2cm thick and trimmed of all but a thin layer of fat

sea salt

One hour before the chops are to be cooked, put the oil in a shallow dish wide enough to hold them in a single layer. Add the garlic, herbs, and lemon juice. Grind a dusting of black pepper on both sides of the chops, then put them into the dish and turn to coat them with the oil. Leave for 1 hour, turning once or twice during this time, so that they are well and truly steeped in it.

15 minutes before serving time, heat broiler on high for 3 minutes. Arrange the chops on the rack of a broiler pan. Put the pan 4in/10cm below the source of heat and broil the chops for 5 minutes on each side, or until they are a rich brown color. Season with freshly ground sea salt.

VARIATION
Omit the basil and rosemary and use 1 tablespoon of tarragon mustard and 2 tablespoons of chopped, fresh tarragon (or 2 teaspoons of the dried herb).

PATLICAN KEBABI

SERVES 6
KEEPS FOR 2 DAYS IN THE FRIDGE | FREEZES FOR 3 MONTHS

Lamb chops from the shoulder are meaty and flavorful, and though not quite tender enough to grill, they melt in the mouth when braised in a savory sauce. This dish from Turkey uses a most delicious combination of spices that marries particularly well with the eggplant to make a really succulent dish for a buffet or an informal dinner.

1 lb/450g eggplants

3½ tsp salt

6 lamb shoulder chops, about 6oz/175g each in weight

5 grinds of black pepper

2 tbsp oil, plus more for frying

1 onion, finely chopped

1 fat garlic clove, chopped

1⅔ cups/400ml vegetable stock

2 tbsp tomato paste

2 tsp brown sugar

1 tsp ground cumin

1 tsp ground cinnamon

cooked rice or bulgar, to serve

Cut the eggplants into 1 in/2.5cm cubes, cover with water plus 3 teaspoons of the salt, and set aside for 30 minutes.

Meanwhile, lightly season the chops with the remaining salt and the pepper, then heat the oil in a large frying pan and brown the meat quickly on both sides. Lift out with a slotted spoon and drain on paper towels. In the same oil, cook the onion over moderate heat until a rich golden brown, then add all the remaining ingredients except the eggplants and the frying oil, stir well, and bring to a boil. Simmer, uncovered, for 5 minutes.

Preheat the oven to 300°F/150°C. Put the meat in an oven-to-table lidded casserole dish, pour over the bubbling sauce, cover, and cook in the slow oven for 1½ hours until very tender.

Meanwhile, squeeze out as much moisture as possible from the eggplants and dry with paper towels. Deep-fry in 2 batches at 325°F/170°C (medium setting) for 5 minutes, then lift out on to paper towels. (If you don't have a deep-fryer, fry the cubes in ¼ cup/60ml oil in a covered frying pan for 10–15 minutes, or until soft and golden.) Add the fried eggplant to the casserole, re-cover, and cook for a further 30 minutes. Serve with rice or bulgar.

GREEK-JEWISH
LAMB FRICASSÉE

SERVES 6–8

KEEPS FOR 3 DAYS IN THE FRIDGE | FREEZES FOR 3 MONTHS

This Greco-Jewish casserole is by tradition cooked the stovetop. If you're around the house, it's quite pleasant to do it this way, giving the pot a stir every now and again—it doesn't take more than 1 hour. If it's more convenient to cook it in the oven, it will take 1½–2 hours.

6 lamb neck steaks, about 6oz/175g each, or 2½–3lb/1.25kg boneless lamb shoulder, cut into 1½in/3cm cubes

scant ¼ cup/1oz/25g flour

1 tsp salt

15 grinds of black pepper

2 tbsp dried mint

3 tbsp olive oil

1 large onion, finely chopped

2 garlic cloves, finely chopped

1 cup/225ml dry white wine or chicken stock (see page 176)

1 tbsp lemon juice

2 tsp sugar

½lb/225g tiny button mushrooms, wiped

½lb/225g thin green beans, such as French beans or haricots verts

basmati rice cooked with 2 cardamom pods (see page 70), or boiled baby potatoes, to serve

Coat the lamb with flour seasoned with the salt, pepper, and half of the dried mint. Heat the oil in a large pan and sauté the onion and garlic until a pale gold color. Add the meat and sauté until a rich brown color. Add the wine or chicken stock and lemon juice and bubble for 3 minutes to concentrate the flavor, then add the sugar and mushrooms.

Simmer for 1 hour on the stovetop or 1½ hours in a slow-moderate oven, 325°F/170°C.

About 20 minutes before the end of the cooking time add the raw beans, stir well, and continue to cook until tender.

Serve with basmati rice flavored as it cooks with 2 cardamom pods or with baby potatoes cooked in their skins. The casserole reheats well.

VARIATION

Use 8oz/225g frozen peas instead of the beans, and add them 10 minutes before the end of cooking time.

KOFTA KEBABS
IN WARM PITA BREAD

SERVES 6

Ground lamb kebabs, seasoned with mint and spices and grilled on skewers, are popular throughout North Africa, the Balkans, and the Middle East. Serve freshly cooked.

FOR THE KOFTA

1 small bunch of parsley (about 1 1/2 oz/40g)

1 garlic clove

1 1/2 lb/675g lean, finely ground lamb

1 large thick slice (about 2oz/50g) white or brown bread, torn up

1 onion, quartered

1 1/2 tsp dried mint

1 tsp ground coriander

1 tsp ground cumin

1 tsp salt

10 grinds of black pepper

FOR THE SALAD

1/2 lb/225g white cabbage

1 carrot

1 sweet red pepper

1 tsp sweet chili sauce

TO SERVE

6 pita breads

12 thinly sliced red onion rings

To make the kofta, put the parsley and garlic in the food processor and pulse until finely chopped. Add all the remaining ingredients, then pulse until the meat is finely chopped and the mixture just clings together. Knead well with your hands to make a smooth, elastic mixture. Shape it into 12 ovals, thread each onto a flat metal skewer, then squeeze firmly around the skewer until about 6in/15cm long and fairly flat. Chill for at least 2 hours, or overnight.

Shred the cabbage finely, coarsely grate the carrot, and cut the pepper into fine strips, then mix all 3 together with the chili sauce.

Cook the kebabs in a hot barbecue or broiler for about 10 minutes, turning frequently. Dip the pita breads briefly into cold water and put them on the grill for about 30 seconds on each side, or until puffed. Slit each bread open lengthways and spoon some of the salad inside. Slide the kebabs off of the skewers and put 2 inside each pita with a few onion rings.

DUTCH MEATBALLS WITH EGG AND LEMON SAUCE

SERVES 3–4
LEFTOVERS KEEP 24 HOURS IN THE FRIDGE
MEATBALLS AND STOCK (NOT SAUCE) FREEZE FOR 3 MONTHS

FOR THE MEATBALLS

1 lb/450g ground veal

1 tbsp chopped parsley

1 onion, finely chopped

finely grated zest of 1 lemon

1 egg, beaten

$\frac{1}{2}$ tsp salt

pinch of white pepper

$\frac{1}{4}$ cup/1oz/25g matzo meal or scant $\frac{1}{2}$ cup/1oz/25g fresh breadcrumbs

FOR THE STEWING LIQUID

1 large onion, sliced

$\frac{1}{2}$ tsp salt

1 pinch of white pepper

1 bay leaf

FOR THE SAUCE

2 tsp cornstarch

$\frac{1}{4}$ cup/50ml lemon juice

2 eggs

2 tsp sugar

Mix all the meatball ingredients together with a fork, then leave to stand for half an hour. Roll into balls the size of a walnut.

In an 8in/20cm saucepan, bring 1$\frac{1}{4}$ cups/275ml water to a boil with the stewing ingredients, then add the meatballs—they should be barely covered by the liquid; if not, add a little extra water. Bring back to a boil, then reduce the heat until the liquid is barely bubbling. Cover and simmer for 45 minutes.

Discard the bay leaf, then lift out the meatballs and onion slices with a slotted spoon and set aside. Bubble the liquid until it has reduced to 1 cup/225ml. Pour into a jug and rinse out the pan.

Put the cornstarch into a bowl and gradually stir in the lemon juice, then whisk in the eggs, sugar, and cooking liquid until smooth, or process for 10 seconds in a food processor. Return to the pan and stir with a wooden spoon over low heat until the sauce thickens enough to coat the back of the spoon.

Alternatively, to cook the sauce in a microwave, mix the sauce ingredients in a microwave-safe jug. Cook on 30 percent (300W) power for 2 minutes, stir well, and cook for a further 2–3 minutes until thickened to coating consistency. Return the sauce to the pan.

Add the meatballs and onion slices to the sauce and heat through until steaming—do not let it come to a boil or it may curdle. Taste and add a little more sugar if too acidic.

FISH

"FRIED" FISH

SERVES 4

COOKED IN OIL KEEPS FOR 3 DAYS IN THE FRIDGE | FREEZES FOR 2 MONTHS

This baked recipe is a great way to serve hot "fried" fish without being tied to the stove or filling the house with the odor of hot oil. It also ensures that the very minimum of oil is absorbed.

1¼–1½ cups /4–6oz/125–175g breadcrumbs or matzo meal

1 tsp salt, plus more to salt the fish

4 fillets or steaks of any white fish

1 egg

¼ cup/60ml sunflower or vegetable oil or 2 tbsp/1oz/25g melted butter

Preheat the oven to 400°F/200°C. Put the crumbs or matzo meal in the oven to brown as it heats up, taking them out when they are well colored.

Wash and salt the fish and set aside to drain. Beat the egg with the oil and 1 teaspoon salt and put in a shallow casserole dish. Have ready a piece of wax paper with the coating crumbs on it. Dry each piece of fish thoroughly with paper towels, then brush with the egg mixture and coat with the crumbs. Arrange the coated fish side by side on flat baking trays (no need to grease them). Leave in a cool place until required.

Put all the fish in the oven and allow to cook, without turning, for 20–25 minutes, depending on the thickness. Serve hot.

GEFILTE FISH PROVENÇALE

ALLOW 1–2 PATTIES PER SERVING
KEEPS FOR 4 DAYS IN THE FRIDGE

Gefilte fish was originally a dish of freshwater fish stuffed with a forcemeat made from chopped or ground fish. Today, patties or balls of sea fish are cooked in stock rather than as a stuffing. The patties in this recipe are poached in a delicious tomato and pepper sauce and can be served either warm or chilled.

TO MAKE 12 PATTIES

1 lb/450g hake fillet, skinned

1 lb/450g haddock fillet, skinned

2 tsp salt, plus extra to salt the fish

1 onion, cut into 1 in/2cm chunks

2 eggs

1 pinch of white pepper

2 tsp sugar

1 tbsp oil

½ cup/2oz/50g medium matzo meal, plus more if needed

FOR THE SAUCE

1 tbsp olive oil

1 onion, finely chopped

15oz/425g can or jar of crushed or puréed tomatoes

2 tbsp ketchup

1 orange or yellow pepper, seeded and thinly sliced

1 tsp salt

1 tsp brown sugar

10 grinds of black pepper

1 bay leaf

½ tsp dried herbes de Provence

Wash and salt the fish and leave to drain. Put the onion into a food processor, together with the eggs, salt, pepper, sugar, and oil, then process to a smooth purée. Pour this purée into a large bowl and stir in the matzo meal, then set aside to swell.

Working in batches, process the fish in the food processor for 5 seconds until finely chopped, then add it to the egg and onion purée and blend in using a large fork. Once all the fish has been processed, mix thoroughly. The mixture should be firm enough to shape into a soft patty. If it feels too "cloggy," stir in 1 or 2 tablespoons of water. If it feels very soft, stir in 1 or 2 tablespoons of the matzo meal. Set aside for half an hour, or overnight in the fridge, if preferred.

Preheat the oven to 300°F/150°C. With wet hands, form the mixture into oval patties, each about 2½in/7cm long, 1½in/4cm wide, and ¾in/2cm thick. Cover and set aside.

To make the sauce, heat the oil and saute the onion until soft and transparent, then add all the remaining ingredients and bubble until reduced to a thick coating consistency.

Arrange the fish patties in a shallow ovenproof dish, pour on the sauce, and loosely cover with foil. Bake for 1 hour, basting the patties once or twice with the sauce.

GRILLED HERRINGS WITH FRESH APPLE SAUCE

SERVES 4
LEFTOVERS AND SAUCE KEEP FOR 4 DAYS IN THE FRIDGE
SAUCE FREEZES FOR 3 MONTHS

Fine, fat fillets of fresh herring, grilled until the flesh is creamy and firm in texture, make a wonderful mid-week meal. The piquant sauce helps to neutralize the natural oiliness of this most nourishing of fish. Since there are special seasons when herrings are in their prime, consult your fishmonger before you buy.

4–6 fresh herring fillets cut from a 12–14oz/ 350–450g fish

salt

FOR THE SAUCE

nut butter or margarine

¾lb/350g tart cooking apples or Granny Smiths, peeled, cored, and roughly chopped

1 tbsp brown sugar

3 tsp creamy horseradish sauce

FOR THE TOPPING

2½ tbsp sunflower oil

4 tsp cider vinegar or red wine vinegar

3 tsp Dijon mustard

2 tsp Worcestershire sauce

1 tsp light soy sauce

½ tsp sea salt

15 grinds of black pepper

First, make the sauce by melting some butter in a small pan and adding the apple, sugar, and 2 teaspoons water. Cover and simmer gently until the apples are very soft, then beat to a purée with a wooden spoon, immersion blender, or food processor. Stir in the creamy horseradish and set aside.

Wash the fish, salt lightly, and leave in a colander to drain for 10 minutes.

Meanwhile, mix the topping ingredients together in a small bowl.

Lightly grease a broiler pan and heat it up 3in/7.5cm from the heat source for 3 minutes. Then lay the fish fillets in it, side by side, skin-side down, and brush them thickly with the topping mixture. Broil for 10 minutes until the fish is a rich brown color. Serve immediately, accompanied by the apple sauce at room temperature.

GOLDEN FILLETS OF MACKEREL WITH A CLEMENTINE AND CUCUMBER SALAD

This is a fish dish to choose if you're looking for a rich taste and satisfying texture without a stratospheric price. Mackerel has a high oil content, and though this is excellent from a health perspective, it does need to be tempered by some kind of acidity, provided here by the tangy salad and delicious marinade. I like to serve this dish with crisp baked potatoes.

6 split mackerel fillets cut from 3 whole fish (each fish should weigh 12–14 oz/350–400g)

salt

FOR THE MARINADE

2 tbsp soy sauce

2 tbsp fresh orange juice

1 tbsp sun-dried tomato or regular tomato paste

1 tbsp chopped parsley

1 garlic clove, chopped

2 tsp Worcestershire sauce

2 tsp lemon juice

15 grinds of black pepper

FOR THE SALAD

3 tbsp sugar

3 tbsp boiling water

1/3 cup/75ml cider vinegar

1/4 cup/1/2 oz/10g chopped dill

10 grinds of black pepper

1 cucumber, thinly sliced

6 clementines, peeled and sectioned

Wash and lightly salt the mackerel fillets, then lay them side by side in a heatproof dish suitable for the oven. Mix together the marinade ingredients, then spoon or brush over the fish in an even layer. Allow to marinate at room temperature for 1 hour.

To make the salad, put the sugar in a small bowl, add the boiling water, and stir until dissolved. Then stir in the vinegar, dill, and black pepper. Pour this over the thinly sliced cucumber and the clementines in a shallow dish and set aside for at least 1 hour before serving.

To cook the fish, preheat the broiler and broil the fillets 4in/10cm from the heat source for 9–10 minutes, or until it is firm to the touch and flakes easily.

The grilled fish is equally delicious served hot, or at room temperature as part of a cold buffet.

POACHED SALMON 3 WAYS

TO POACH SALMON FILLETS ON THE STOVE

KEEPS FOR 3 DAYS IN THE FRIDGE | FREEZES FOR 3 MONTHS

Place the washed and salted fish on a double piece of parchment paper or foil greased with a little oil, then fold into a parcel, securing it, if necessary, with loosely tied string. Put it in a pan and cover with cold water. Add 2 teaspoons salt and a pinch of pepper and bring slowly to a boil.

To serve hot Reduce the heat and allow to simmer (but never boil) for 6 minutes for each 1lb/450g, plus 6 minutes extra. Lift out, drain well, unwrap, and serve.

To serve cold When the water comes to a boil, bubble for 3 minutes only, then remove from the heat and leave the fish in the covered pan until the liquid is cold—at least 3 hours. It can be kept in the liquid for up to 3 days in the fridge.

TO POACH SALMON STEAKS ON THE STOVE

Lightly butter a large frying pan. Lay the salmon steaks on the pan and add ¾ cup/175ml water or fish stock for 4 steaks, or 1½ cups/350ml for 8 steaks. Bring to simmering point, cover, and simmer—never boil—for 10 minutes, turning the fish once.

TO POACH SALMON STEAKS IN THE MICROWAVE

SERVES 4
KEEPS FOR 3 DAYS IN THE FRIDGE | LEFTOVERS FREEZE FOR 3 MONTHS

4 salmon steaks, about 6oz/175g each

²/₃ cup/150ml fish stock

squeeze of lemon juice

salt

white pepper

Arrange the washed steaks around the edge of a round microwave-safe dish, with the thin part of the steaks at the center. Pour on the stock and lemon juice and cover, then cook on 60 percent (600W) power for 6 minutes, turning the fish over after 3 minutes. Leave to stand for 5 minutes, then sprinkle lightly with salt and pepper.

FILLETS OF SALMON WITH
A CRUSHED PECAN CRUST

SERVES 6–8
SERVE THE SAME DAY

butter, for greasing

1²/₃lb/750g thick salmon fillet, cut into 6–8 pieces

salt

white pepper

2 tbsp reduced-calorie mayonnaise

FOR THE CRUST

1²/₃ cups/6½oz/185g shelled pecans

¼ cup/10g snipped chives

2 tbsp/1oz/30g unsalted butter, melted

First, make the crust. In the food processor, pulse the nuts until coarsely ground, then mix with the chives and melted butter in a small bowl.

Lightly grease a shallow baking pan wide enough to hold the pieces of salmon in one layer. Arrange them in this dish and season lightly with the salt and pepper, then spread the surface with a thin layer of mayonnaise and cover completely with the nut mixture, patting it on well. Set aside until ready to cook.

About 15 minutes before serving, preheat the oven to 425°F/220°C. Put the salmon in the oven for 8–10 minutes, or until the salmon flakes easily with a fork. Serve warm.

SALMON KEDGEREE

SERVES 4
KEEPS FOR 2 DAYS IN THE FRIDGE | DO NOT FREEZE

A delicious variation of the classic British-Indian recipe, this can be served as a main course for 4 or as an appetizer for 6.

1 tbsp sunflower or vegetable oil

1 shallot or 1 small bunch of scallions (white parts), finely chopped

1¼ cups/8oz/225g basmati rice

¼ cup/50ml dry white wine (optional)

2½ cups/575ml fish stock, or water mixed with 1 fish bouillon cube

1 tbsp lemon juice

½ tsp salt

8 grinds of black pepper

½lb/225g raw salmon fillet, skinned

4 hard-boiled eggs, shelled and roughly chopped or quartered

2 tbsp/1oz/30g butter or margarine

1 tbsp chopped parsley

¼ cup/1oz/25g sliced almonds

In an 8in/20cm lidded frying pan, heat the oil and fry the shallots or scallions until very soft and creamy gold in color, then add the rice and toss over high heat for 1 minute. Add the wine (if using) and bubble until it has almost evaporated, then add the stock, lemon juice, salt, and pepper, and bring to a boil. Cover tightly and simmer gently for 15–20 minutes until the rice is bite-tender (taste it).

Cut the salmon into ½in/1cm chunks and add to the rice, cover, and cook for a further 5 minutes over gentle heat, stirring occasionally, until the fish is cooked.

Stir in half of the the eggs, the butter or margarine, and the parsley, and gently mix with a fork. Turn into a heatproof serving dish and sprinkle with the almonds (or you can toast the almonds separately and serve them alongside, if preferred).

Just before serving, put it in a preheated broiler for 2 minutes until golden brown. Garnish with the remaining chopped eggs.

SAMAK KEBAB

SERVES 6

KEEPS FOR 1 DAY IN THE FRIDGE | DO NOT FREEZE

For this recipe I have borrowed a Turkish way of marinating fish in a spicy sauce. The marinade softens the texture of the fish, while the spices add extra zing. Kebabs prepared by this method are best hot out of the oven or barbecue, but they're still delicious eaten at room temperature up to an hour after cooking. Serve them with rice and potatoes and a mixed salad.

2lb/900g thick fillets of firm white fish (halibut, sea bass, haddock, or cod), skinned

¼ cup/60ml olive oil

FOR THE MARINADE

2 large onions

½ cup/120ml lemon juice

2 tsp ground cumin

2 fat garlic cloves, finely chopped

1 tsp paprika

1 tsp sea salt

20 grinds of black pepper

TO SERVE

coarsely chopped parsley

lemon wedges

paprika

Cut the fish into 1in/2.5cm cubes and arrange in one layer in a shallow dish.

To make the marinade, peel and grate the onions and extract the juice by pressing them through a sieve into a small bowl. Mix the onion juice with the remaining marinade ingredients. Pour this marinade over the fish and set aside for at least an hour, turning 2–3 times.

Thread the fish on to metal or soaked wooden skewers and brush all over with the olive oil. The dish can be prepared to this stage early in the day. To cook, broil or grill for 6–8 minutes until golden, turning frequently.

To serve, sprinkle the coarsely chopped parsley on an oval fish platter, lay the fish on top, and garnish with the lemon wedges and a dusting of paprika.

GRILLED TROUT
WITH SESAME SAUCE

SERVES 4

4 whole trout, each weighing about 8–12oz/ 225–350g, gutted and cleaned but with the head left on (this keeps it moist)

oil, for brusing

FOR THE SAUCE

2 tbsp/1oz/30g butter

1 tbsp sesame oil

2 tbsp white sesame seeds

¼ cup/60ml fresh lemon juice

scant ½ cup/100ml fish or vegetable stock

1 pinch of salt

1 small pinch of white pepper

Lightly brush the the skin of the fish with oil.

Heat your grill or broiler to medium, and grill or broil the fish for 5–10 minutes on each side, depending on the thickness (a fish 1½in/4cm thick will take 15–18 minutes in total). Test by removing a little skin to see if the fish flakes easily with a fork.

In a small saucepan, melt the butter and sesame oil, then add the sesame seeds and sauté gently until they are golden brown, tossing them in the pan several times. Add the remaining ingredients and bring to a boil, then simmer until the liquid is reduced by half. When the fish are cooked, transfer to individual plates and remove the skin. Reheat the sauce and spoon over the fish. Serve at once.

VEGETABLE AND SIDE DISHES

ISRAELI FRUITED WINTER SALAD

SERVES 6
SERVE THE SAME DAY

A refreshing green salad to serve either as an appetizer or for a buffet.

½ cup/2oz/50g blanched almond halves

½ iceberg lettuce, shredded

4in/10cm piece of Napa cabbage, finely sliced, or any preferred salad greens

6oz/175g seedless black grapes

FOR THE DRESSING

⅓ cup/75ml sunflower oil

2 tbsp extra virgin olive oil

1 tbsp red wine or raspberry vinegar

1 tbsp fresh lemon juice

1 tsp sugar

½ tsp whole-grain mustard

½ tsp sea salt

8 grinds of black pepper

Shake all the dressing ingredients together in a screw-top jar until slightly thickened, then chill until serving.

Toast and lightly salt the blanched almonds.

Arrange the finely shredded lettuce and cabbage or other greens in a wide salad bowl, cover, and chill until ready to serve. Shortly before serving, add the halved grapes and the almonds and toss with the dressing.

ISRAELI SALAD

SERVES 6
SERVE THE SAME DAY

This is the archetypal Middle Eastern salad, served at breakfast, lunch, and dinner. Whether it's prepared for 200 kibbutzniks or by street vendors who spoon it into your pita bread along with their freshly fried falafel balls, it's always made with cubed vegetables—cucumber, tomato, and peppers, cut large or small, according to the patience of the cook. This makes a refreshing side for grilled dishes, whether meat or fish, but it's equally good with cold poultry and meats.

1 red bell pepper

1 green bell pepper

3 large, firm, preferably vine-ripened, tomatoes

1 cucumber, unpeeled

1 tsp coarse salt

FOR THE DRESSING

¼ cup/60ml sunflower oil

1 tbsp fruity olive oil

1 tbsp wine vinegar

1 tbsp lemon juice

1 fat garlic clove, crushed

1 tsp salt

10 grinds of black pepper

1 tsp superfine sugar

1 tbsp finely snipped fresh mint or 1 tsp dried mint

2 tbsp chopped parsley

All the salad ingredients and the dressing can be prepared up to a day ahead, if you wish, but it is best to combine them an hour before serving to retain the characteristic crispness.

Halve and deseed the peppers and remove the white pith. Cut each of the vegetables into even ¾in/2cm cubes or squares, then put the tomatoes and peppers into separate bowls, cover, and chill until ready to serve. Put the cucumber cubes into a salad spinner or sieve, sprinkle with the coarse salt, and set aside for 30 minutes, then spin or drain and refrigerate until serving.

In a screw-top jar, shake together all the dressing ingredients except the fresh herbs. Add the dried mint, if using, then set aside for several hours to mature in flavor. Put the cucumber, pepper, and tomato cubes into a large bowl, then stir in the chopped parsley and mint and the dressing, and mix well using 2 spoons. Arrange the salad in a fairly shallow dish—it looks particularly effective against black or white. This is best served cool but not cold.

HUNGARIAN CUCUMBER SALAD

SERVES 6
KEEPS FOR 2 DAYS IN THE FRIDGE | DO NOT FREEZE

An excellent salad for a low-calorie diet, since no oil is used in the dressing. Although not traditional, the salad looks pretty with a mixture of baby red and yellow tomatoes.

I cucumber

12oz/350g small tomatoes

I large red pepper

3 tsp kosher salt

FOR THE DRESSING

2 tsp sugar or other granular sweetener

I tbsp hot water

¼ cup/60ml wine vinegar

15 grinds of black pepper

I tsp salt

I tbsp chopped dill, chives, or mint

Make the salad at least 2 or 3 hours before serving to allow the flavor to develop. Slice the cucumber as thinly as possible. Cut the tomatoes in halves or quarters according to size. Halve, deseed, and remove the white pith from the pepper, then cut the flesh in thin strips. Put the cucumber slices and tomatoes in a bowl, sprinkle with salt, and set aside for an hour.

Put the sugar in a bowl, pour on the hot water, stir well, then add all the remaining dressing ingredients. (If using an alternative granular sweetener, dissolve in cold water.)

Lift out the tomatoes and cucumber slices with a slotted spoon and discard the liquid that has come out of them, then return them to the bowl and add the peppers. Pour the dressing over the vegetables and toss them together gently. Transfer to a serving dish and chill until required.

KATSIS KISHUIM

SERVES 4–6 AS AN APPETIZER, 6–8 AS A DIP
KEEPS FOR 3 DAYS IN THE FRIDGE | DO NOT FREEZE

This Israeli zucchini pâté is light on the tongue, with a delicate but intriguing flavor—no one can guess the main ingredient without asking. It makes an excellent vegetarian alternative to chopped liver.

2 tbsp/1oz/30g butter

1 small onion, thinly sliced

1 lb 2oz/500g zucchinis, thinly sliced

½ tsp fine sea salt

8 grinds of black pepper

1 pinch of cayenne pepper or hot chili powder

1 sprig of parsley

2 hard-boiled eggs, shelled and quartered

Melt the butter and sauté the onion over moderate heat until it has turned a rich gold, then add the zucchini, salt, pepper, and chili powder and toss well. When the zucchini slices begin to color, cover and steam them over low heat, shaking the pan occasionally until they feel tender when pierced with a sharp knife, about 5–6 minutes.

Pulse the parsley in a food processor, then add the hard-boiled egg quarters with the vegetables and juices and process until the mixture becomes a smooth pâté. Turn into a terrine or pottery bowl, cover, and chill for several hours, then leave at room temperature for half an hour before serving.

AVOCADO AND EGG PÂTÉ

SERVES 4 AS AN APPETIZER, 6 AS A DIP
KEEPS FOR 2 DAYS IN THE FRIDGE | DO NOT FREEZE

Another favorite Israeli appetizer. There is a strong affinity with the egg and scallion forspeise (see page 23), but this has the added richness of avocados to give it a different flavor and texture.

1/2 large bunch of parsley

1/2 small bunch of scallions

2 ripe avocados, peeled, pitted, and roughly cubed

1 tbsp lemon juice

2 hard-boiled eggs, shelled and halved

1 tsp fine sea salt

5 grinds of black pepper

1 tbsp mayonnaise

chips, crackers, or challah, to serve

Finely chop the parsley and the scallions in a food processor. Add the avocados and the lemon juice, then add the eggs, salt, and pepper. Pulse until the eggs are finely chopped.

Turn into a bowl and mix in enough of the mayonnaise to bind the mixture into a pâté. Taste and re season if necessary. Pile into a shallow bowl and chill until required. Serve with chips, crackers, or spread on fingers of challah.

CAPONATA ALLA SICILIANA

SERVES 6

KEEPS FOR 3 DAYS IN THE FRIDGE | DO NOT FREEZE

According to the Sicilian cookbook *Sicilia e le Isole in bocca*, this rich and wonderful eggplant stew—a culinary relative of French ratatouille—originated in the Mafia port of Palermo. Serve with plenty of brown or rye country bread to mop up the delicious juices.

I heaped tbsp salt

2lb/900g thin eggplants, unpeeled and cut into ¾in/2cm cubes

½ cup/125ml olive oil

2 garlic cloves, finely chopped

⅓ cup/75ml good-quality extra virgin olive oil

2 onions, finely sliced

1 celery heart (6–8 stalks), sliced ½in/1cm thick

15oz/425g canned chopped tomatoes, well drained

2 cups/8oz/225g large black olives, pitted and sliced

2 tbsp capers in brine, well drained

2 tbsp granulated sugar or other granular sweetener

¼ cup/60ml white wine vinegar

1 tsp freeze-dried basil

TO SERVE

sea salt

15 grinds of black pepper

tiny sprigs or leaves of fresh herbs—cilantro, parsley, or basil

Half-fill a salad spinner with cold water, add the salt and then the eggplants, cover, and leave for 30 minutes. Pour off the water, then spin dry.

Heat the olive oil in a large lidded sauté pan, add the well-dried eggplants and the garlic, toss to coat with the oil, and cover. Allow to brown and soften for 20 minutes, stirring 2 or 3 times. Remove with a slotted spoon.

Meanwhile, heat the extra virgin oil in an 8in/20cm pan, put in the onions, stir well, cover, and cook gently until golden and softened. Add the celery and cook for a further 5 minutes, then add all the remaining ingredients except the eggplants and cook, uncovered, until thick and juicy.

Stir in the sautéed eggplants, tossing carefully to mix all the ingredients thoroughly. Chill for several hours, or overnight. Season with sea salt and freshly ground black pepper, then sprinkle with the herbs before serving.

OMELETTE BASQUAISE

SERVES 4
SERVE HOT OFF THE PAN

4 tbsp/2oz/60g butter

2 tsp olive oil

1 small onion, finely chopped

1 red pepper, deseeded and cubed

2 mushrooms, sliced

3 fresh or canned tomatoes, chopped

1 small garlic clove, crushed

1 tsp dried oregano

1 tsp chopped parsley

salt and black pepper

6 eggs, beaten with ½ tsp salt and 8 grinds of black pepper

½ cup/2oz/50g grated mature Cheddar cheese

Melt the butter with the oil in an 8in/20cm oven-safe omelet pan, then add the onion. Sauté gently for 5 minutes, then add the red pepper, mushrooms, tomatoes, garlic, oregano, parsley, salt, and black pepper.

Cover and cook for 10 minutes until soft, then uncover and pour in the eggs. Stir well, then cook until set and golden brown underneath. Sprinkle with the grated cheese, then place the pan very briefly under a hot boriler until the top is melted and golden. Serve at once from the dish.

BADINJAN KUKU
PERSIAN EGGPLANT FRITATTA

SERVES 4
SERVE HOT OFF THE PAN

2 eggplants

salt

¼ cup/60ml extra virgin olive oil

1 large beefsteak tomato, finely sliced

1 small onion, finely chopped

1 garlic clove, finely chopped

2½ tbsp finely chopped fresh dill or parsley

2½ tbsp raisins

pinch of ground saffron (optional)

10 grinds of black pepper

1 tsp salt

6 large eggs, beaten

Cut the eggplants into roughly 1 in/2.5cm chunks, put on a large plate or in a salad spinner, and sprinkle liberally with salt. After 30 minutes, rinse well with cold water, drain thoroughly, and dry (this reduces the amount of oil needed for frying).

Heat the oil in a large oven-safe frying pan, add the well-dried eggplant chunks, the tomato, onion, and garlic, and sauté gently for 5 minutes. Stir in the dill or parsley, raisins, saffron, black pepper, and salt.

Pour in the eggs. Stir well, then cook until set and golden brown underneath. If you like, place the pan very briefly under a hot broiler until the top is set and golden. Serve at once from the dish.

PIPERRADA

SERVES 4
SERVE HOT OFF THE PAN

Though capsicums are native to Mexico and Central America, they have been a mainstay of Sephardi and Ashkenazi cuisine for centuries. A point of interest: weight for weight, peppers contain between 6 and 9 times the Vitamin C of tomatoes, and contain only 78 calories per 3½oz/100g—the weight of an average pepper.

⅓ cup/75ml extra virgin olive oil

2 onions, thinly sliced

2 garlic cloves, finely chopped

2 large, very ripe beefsteak tomatoes, halved, deseeded, and sectioned

2 yellow peppers, deseeded and cut into thin strips

2 red peppers, deseeded and cut into thin strips

sea salt

black pepper

6 eggs

Heat the oil in a large lidded frying pan. Add the onions and garlic and sauté, covered, until softened and golden. Add the tomatoes and peppers to the pan and simmer gently, uncovered, for 10–12 minutes until the peppers are softened but still slightly firm. Uncover, reduce the heat, and season to taste with salt and pepper.

Beat the eggs just to blend, then pour over the pepper mixture. Cook very gently for several minutes, or long enough for the eggs to begin to set but still be very creamy. Slide on to a warm serving dish.

Preheat the oven to 325°F/160°C and oil an oven-safe pan or gratin dish about 10in/25cm in diameter or a baking pan approximately 11 x 7in/28 x 18cm. Stir the vegetable mixture into the eggs, turn into the baking pan or dish, and cook, uncovered, for 35–40 minutes, or until firm to a gentle touch. Leave to cool for a couple of minutes before cutting. Serve at once.

IMAM BAYELDI

SERVES 6
KEEPS FOR 3 DAYS IN THE FRIDGE | DO NOT FREEZE

The following recipe is how the Turks make this rich, luscious baked eggplant dish, though different versions are served all over the Middle East.

6 small, oval eggplants, each weighing about ½lb/225g

½ tsp salt, plus more to salt the eggplant

2 large onions

3 tbsp extra virgin olive oil

15oz/425g can whole tomatoes, drained and chopped

2 tbsp currants

½ tsp ground cinnamon

½ tsp ground cumin

1 tsp brown sugar

10 grinds of black pepper

3 tbsp chopped parsley

FOR THE SAUCE

½ cup/125ml hot water

¼ cup/60ml extra virgin olive oil

2½ tbsp lemon juice

2 tsp brown sugar

1 garlic clove, halved

TO SERVE

crusty bread or warm pita bread

Cut a deep slit lengthways in the center of each eggplant, sprinkle inside with salt, and set aside for 30 minutes. Squeeze out any black juices, rinse under cold water, and pat dry.

Slice the onions finely, then sauté gently in the olive oil until soft and golden. Add the tomatoes, currants, spices, sugar, pepper, and ½ teaspoon salt and simmer gently until the mixture is thick but still juicy. Add the parsley and allow to cool.

Use the cooled mixture to stuff the slits in each eggplant. Arrange the eggplants side by side in a shallow casserole dish or Dutch oven, slit-side up, and add the sauce ingredients—first the water and olive oil, then pour over the lemon juice and sprinkle with the sugar. Add the garlic.

Cover the dish and simmer very gently, either on the stovetop or in the oven at 325°F/160°C, for 1½ hours, or until quite soft and most of the liquid has been absorbed. Chill, preferably overnight.

When you are ready, lift the eggplants from the sauce, spoon a little sauce over each one, and serve at room temperature with crusty bread or warm pita.

EGYPTIAN-JEWISH STUFFED EGGPLANTS

SERVES 6

KEEPS FOR 3 DAYS IN THE FRIDGE | FREEZES FOR 3 MONTHS

This is the way Egyptian Jews prepare stuffed eggplants. It is one of my favorite stuffed vegetable recipes. The dish reheats well.

3 glossy boat-shaped eggplants, each weighing about ½lb/225g, or 6 long, slender ones

¼ cup/50ml sunflower or other flavorless oil for frying (add extra if required)

flour, for coating

FOR THE STUFFING

1 lb/450g ground beef

1 egg, beaten

1 tsp salt

10 grinds of black pepper

1 tsp paprika

⅓ cup/2oz/60g uncooked rice

FOR THE SAUCE

½ onion, finely chopped

14oz/400g canned chopped Italian tomatoes, strained, or passata

¼ cup/2oz/50g brown sugar

juice of 1 large lemon (3 tbsp)

½ tsp salt

1 pinch of white pepper

a little chicken stock or water if necessary

Preheat the oven to 350°F/180°C.

Cut the eggplants in half lengthways and scoop out the flesh, leaving a good ¼in/5mm of eggplant all the way around. Roughly chop the scooped-out eggplant flesh, then fry until soft in a little oil. Add this to the meat in a large bowl, together with all the remaining stuffing ingredients, and mix well. Mound the meat mixture into each eggplant shell, pressing it in firmly.

Dip each stuffed eggplant in flour, then, very carefully, brown it quickly on both sides in a little hot oil. Arrange the browned eggplants in a wide casserole dish.

Start the sauce in the same oil. Cook the chopped onion, covered, until soft and golden brown, then stir in all the remaining ingredients for the sauce. When the sauce is bubbling, pour it around the eggplants—they should be just submerged. If not, top up with a little chicken stock or water.

Cover the casserole and put in the oven for about 30 minutes, until the sauce is bubbling nicely, then turn the oven down to 300°F/150°C and cook for a further 2 hours. When the eggplants are ready, they will have absorbed most of the sauce, leaving just enough to pour over each eggplant when it is served.

FRITADA DE ESPINACA
SEPHARDI SPINACH AND MUSHROOM BAKE

SERVES 4–5 AS A MAIN DISH
SERVE WARM OR AT ROOM TEMPERATURE
KEEPS FOR 2 DAYS IN THE FRIDGE | DO NOT FREEZE

This baked omelet is especially creamy in texture since it is made with a herb or garlic and herb cream cheese. It can be served warm or cold, and frozen uncooked (thaw and bake when required).

8oz/225g package frozen leaf spinach, thawed

2 tbsp/1oz/25g butter or margarine

the bulbs and 3in/7.5cm of stalk from a small bunch of scallions, finely sliced

1¼ cups/4oz/125g mushrooms, finely sliced

3 eggs

about 5oz/150g herbed cream cheese

1½ cups/6oz/175g grated Lancashire or Cheddar cheese (reserve ¼ cup for the topping)

1 tbsp chopped parsley

1 tsp salt

15 grinds of black pepper

Preheat the oven to 375°F/190°C. Grease a rectangular baking dish about 11 x 7in/28 x 18cm and about 3in/7cm deep, or an 8–9in/20–22cm square foil container about 3in/7cm deep.

Put the spinach in a sieve and press out as much moisture as possible, then roughly chop. Heat the butter or margarine in a sauté pan and sauté the onions, covered, until soft and golden. Add the mushrooms and cook over a brisk heat until softened and golden brown. Add the spinach and continue to cook, stirring, until there is no free moisture in the pan—this will take 2–3 minutes.

Whisk the eggs in a small bowl. Put the cream cheese in a larger bowl and stir in the grated cheese, except for the cheese reserved for the topping. Add the eggs, sautéed vegetables, parsley, salt, and pepper.

Pour into the prepared dish and scatter with the reserved cheese. Bake for 25–30 minutes, or until firm to the touch and golden brown.

PASTA WITH A SYRACUSE SAUCE

SERVES 4

KEEPS FOR 3 DAYS IN THE FRIDGE | SAUCE OR LEFTOVERS FREEZE FOR 1 MONTH

The joy of pasta is that it takes so little time to cook, and this dish looks particularly inviting with a mixture of three colors of pasta. Anchovies are always used in Sicily, but if you prefer the sauce to be wholly vegetarian, a tablespoon of drained capers can be added instead. It is traditionally served with a flavorful grated cheese such as Pecorino.

12oz/350g rigatoni or penne (tri-color pasta is prettiest)

salt

finely grated cheese

FOR THE SAUCE

1 lb/450g eggplants, cut into ½in/1cm cubes

1 red pepper

1 yellow pepper

1 tbsp sunflower or vegetable oil

1 tbsp olive oil

2 garlic cloves, finely chopped

15oz/425g canned chopped Italian tomatoes

12 fat black olives, pitted

2oz/50g canned anchovies, drained and cut into ½in/1cm lengths

10 grinds of black pepper

6 basil leaves, coarsely shredded

First, start the sauce. Put the unpeeled eggplant cubes in a salad spinner or colander and sprinkle thickly with salt. Leave for 30 minutes, then rinse well and dry.

Meanwhile, grill or broil the peppers until the skin looks charred, leave them wrapped in paper towels for 5 minutes, then strip off the skin with your fingers and cut the flesh in narrow strips.

In a heavy 9in/23cm saucepan or deep lidded frying pan, heat the oils and sauté the eggplant, covered, for 10 minutes, then uncover and add the pepper strips and all of the remaining sauce ingredients. Cover and simmer gently for 5 minutes, then taste and add a little salt if necessary. The sauce should be thick but juicy.

Meanwhile, cook the pasta according to the package directions, then drain well. Put the hot sauce into a bowl and, using 2 spoons, toss with the hot pasta so that every piece is coated before turning into a warm dish. Serve at once with the grated cheese.

RAW PASTA SAUCES

In these two pasta dishes, the sauce is not cooked. To prepare the first, all you need is a sharp knife, and for the second, a food processor. But because these sauces are only at room temperature, it's essential to heat your serving dish and plates so the pasta doesn't become lukewarm.

SPAGHETTINI WITH BLACK OLIVES

SERVES 2 | MAKE AND EAT THE SAME DAY

5oz/150g spaghettini or spaghetti

salt, for cooking the pasta

1 cup/5oz/150g black olives

1 garlic clove

1 tsp fresh oregano leaves, or ¼ tsp dried

¼ cup/60ml good olive oil

10 grinds of black pepper

1 tbsp/½oz/15g unsalted butter

Cook the pasta according to the packet directions until al dente. While it cooks, cut the olive flesh away from the pit and chop coarsely with a knife. Finely chop the garlic and oregano, then mix with the the olives in a small bowl. Slowly stir in the olive oil and add the pepper. Melt the butter in a large bowl in the microwave. Drain the pasta (leaving some water clinging to it), then add to the butter. Toss well to coat the strands, then add the olive mixture. Toss together and serve.

LINGUINE WITH WALNUT SAUCE

SERVES 6 | MAKE AND EAT THE SAME DAY

1 cup/4oz/125g shelled walnuts

½ small garlic clove, peeled

4 tbsp/2oz/60g butter

scant ½ cup/100ml fromage frais or Greek yogurt

½ tsp salt

15 grinds of black pepper

14 oz/400g fresh linguine

1 cup/3oz/75g freshly grated Parmesan

Make the sauce in a food processor. Blend the walnuts, garlic, butter, fromage frais, salt, and pepper very thoroughly until you have a smooth sauce.

Cook the pasta according to the package directions. Reserve ¼ cup/60ml of the cooking liquid, then drain the pasta lightly in a colander. Add the reserved liquid to the sauce to thin it to coating consistency, then mix it with the pasta. Add the grated Parmesan, toss well together, and serve.

SAUTÉED SWEET PEPPERS

SERVES 4
SERVE HOT OFF THE PAN

Sweet peppers need sun and warmth to mature and sweeten. Whatever the color, the vegetable should be glossy and firm and free of bruises. Before it is used, every scrap of the white ribs and bitter seeds needs to be discarded. This is the simplest—and one of the most delicious—ways to cook peppers.

4 large, glossy bell peppers of any color

2½ tbsp extra virgin olive oil

1 small garlic clove, crushed with salt

1 tbsp chopped oregano, or 1 tsp dried marjoram or oregano

1 tsp salt, if needed

Cut the peppers in half and remove the seeds and ribs. Wash and then slice in strips, 3 to each half. Heat the oil gently, then add the peppers and cook quickly for a few minutes until they begin to soften, stirring frequently. Add the garlic, cover, reduce the heat to the minimum, and cook slowly for 15–20 minutes until tender. Add the herbs and salt.

These are best eaten hot off the pan, since they tend to get soggy if reheated.

VIENNESE BRAISED RED CABBAGE

SERVES 6–8

KEEPS FOR 4 DAYS IN THE FRIDGE | FREEZES FOR 3 MONTHS

Jewish cooks with German and Austrian backgrounds make wonderful variations on the theme of red cabbage, using apples, dried fruit, fruit jelly, vinegar, and wine in different permutations to create the sweet-and-sour effect that's characteristic of this luscious dish.

2lb/900g red cabbage

4 tbsp/2oz/50g butter

1 large onion, finely chopped

2 tbsp brown sugar, plus more to taste (optional)

3½ tbsp crab apple or redcurrant jelly

3 tbsp cider vinegar

1 tbsp water

2 tsp salt

¼ tsp white pepper

1 large bay leaf

Preheat the oven to 375°F/190°C.

Quarter the cabbage, remove and discard the stalk section, then shred finely by hand or in a food processor. Rinse in cold water and drain well.

Melt the butter in a heavy pan large enough to hold the cabbage. Add the onion and cook for 5 minutes until golden brown. Add the sugar, if using, and stir until it begins to caramelize. Now add the cabbage and all the remaining ingredients, stirring well to blend until bubbling. Transfer to a casserole dish—a covered roaster or an enameled steel dish are both excellent.

Cook in the oven for 45 minutes to 1 hour. Stir twice. Taste and add more sugar if necessary—the cabbage should have an equal balance of sour and sweet. It should also have a little bite left when it is ready. It can then be kept hot at 275°F/140°C for as long as required. It also reheats extremely well in the microwave—cover and cook on 100 percent (1000W) power for 2½ minutes or until steaming.

POTATO LATKES

SERVES 4–6 | BEST SERVED HOT OFF THE PAN
KEEPS FOR 2 DAYS IN THE FRIDGE | FREEZES FOR 4 MONTHS

Latkes are fritters that were originally made with cream cheese in honor of Judith, whose heroism is said to have inspired the Maccabees in their rebellion. As Chanukkah falls in December, when fresh milk was scarce, the Jews of Eastern Europe substituted potatoes for cheese.

4 large potatoes, peeled (about 1½lb/675g in weight, to make 2½ cups grated)

½ onion, either cut into 1in/2.5cm chunks (food processor method) or finely sliced (traditional method)

2 eggs

1 tsp salt

pinch of white pepper

4½ tbsp self-rising flour or 4½ tbsp all-purpose flour plus a pinch of baking powder

any flavorless oil, such as sunflower, for frying

Begin the preparation only 15 minutes before cooking to avoid the potatoes turning brown.

Traditional method With a cheese grater, grate the potatoes almost to a pulp. Leave in a sieve to drain for 10 minutes. Put in a bowl and add the remaining ingredients. You are now ready to cook.

Food processor method With some food processor grating discs, the potato pulp will be too coarse, so you may need to pulse briefly after grating, using the metal blade. If you have a fine shredding disk or prefer more rösti-like latkes, omit this stage.

Cut the potatoes to fit the feed tube, then grate through the grating disc. Turn into a metal sieve and press down firmly with a spoon to remove as much moisture as possible. Leave to drain.

Put the onion, eggs, salt, pepper, and flour into the bowl and process with the metal blade until smooth—about 5 seconds. Add the drained potatoes and pulse for 3–4 seconds until the potatoes are finer and are almost reduced to a coarse pulp.

To cook In a large, heavy frying pan, add oil to a depth of ½in/1cm and place over medium heat. When the oil is hot (375°F/190°C), put in tablespoons of the mixture, flattening each latke with the back of a spoon. Cook over steady moderate heat for 5 minutes on each side until a rich brown. Drain on crumpled paper towels, then serve as soon as possible, or keep hot in a moderate oven, 350°F/180°C, for up to 15 minutes.

INDONESIAN STYLE
CORN FRITTERS

SERVES 6 | SERVE HOT OFF THE PAN OR AT ROOM TEMPERATURE
LEFTOVERS KEEP FOR 3 DAYS IN THE FRIDGE | FREEZE FOR 1 MONTH

Corn fritters in a parev version—one that can be eaten both with milk and meat dishes—are generally tasteless and not worth the effort. But that can't be said for this delicious recipe, which I have adapted from Sri Owen's wonderful book on Indonesian food and cooking (also published by Interlink). They also make very interesting finger food for a drinks party.

1 medium eggplant

½ tsp salt, plus more to salt the eggplant

½ cup/250ml sunflower oil

4 shallots, finely chopped

½ tsp chili powder

2 garlic cloves, finely chopped

1 tsp ground coriander

11 oz/325g canned corn, drained

1 egg, beaten

¼ cup/1 oz/35g all-purpose flour

1 tsp baking powder

2½ tbsp thinly sliced scallions

Peel the eggplant and cut into ½in/1 cm cubes, then put in a colander or salad spinner and sprinkle with salt. Leave for 30–40 minutes, then rinse and squeeze as dry as possible.

In a heavy sauté or frying pan, heat 2 tablespoons of the oil and stir-fry the shallots, chili powder, and garlic for 2 minutes. Add the eggplant, stir well, and season with the coriander and ½ teaspoon salt. Simmer together for 4 minutes until the eggplant is tender, then set aside to cool.

Put the corn in a bowl. Add the eggplant mixture and all the remaining ingredients, apart from the rest of the oil, and mix well. Re-season if necessary. Heat the oil in the sauté pan over medium heat and drop the mixture by heaped tablespoons into it (it should sizzle), then flatten each fritter lightly with the back of a fork. Cook for 3 minutes on each side.

Serve hot or at room temperature. You can keep the fritters hot in an oven preheated to 225°F/110°C for up to 30 minutes. Leftover cold fritters can be gently reheated under the broiler.

FLUFFY MASHED POTATOES

SERVES 4–6 | MAKE AND EAT THE SAME DAY

2–3lb/900g–1.5kg potatoes, peeled and quartered

2 tsp salt, plus more if needed

½ cup/125ml hot milk, plus more if needed

4 tbsp/2oz/50g butter

¼ tsp white pepper or 10 grinds of black pepper

¼ tsp freshly grated nutmeg (optional)

Put the potatoes in a large saucepan and cover with boiling water. Add the salt, bring back to a boil, cover, and cook at a steady boil for 15 minutes, or until absolutely tender when pierced with a vegetable knife.

Drain, return to the stove in the same pan, and shake over gentle heat until all the moisture has evaporated. Pour the milk down the side of the pan and when it starts to steam, add the butter, white pepper, and nutmeg, if using. Whisk over very low heat until the potatoes lighten and look fluffy. Add more milk if the mixture seems too dry. Taste and add more salt if necessary. Pile into a warm vegetable dish and serve immediately.

PERFECT ROASTED POTATOES

SERVES 4–6 | SERVE HOT FROM THE OVEN

2–3lb/900g–1.5kg potatoes, peeled and cut into 1in/2.5cm slices

1 tsp salt, plus more to taste

oil

a pat of margarine

325°F/160°C 1¾ hours
350°F/180°C 1½ hours
375°F/190°C 1½ hours
400°F/200°C 1¼ hours
425°F/220°C 1¼ hours

Put the potatoes in a large saucepan half-full of boiling water, add 1 teaspoon salt, and bring slowly back to a boil. Cook until almost but not quite tender—about 15–20 minutes. Drain the potatoes, then return them to the empty saucepan and shake over low heat until absolutely dry.

Meanwhile, preheat the oven to the temperature on the left that is best for whatever else you are cooking. Place a thin layer of oil in the bottom of a shallow roasting pan just large enough to hold the potato slices in one layer, and place this in the oven until the oil is hot.

Put the pan of hot oil on the stove, add the margarine, carefully lay the potatoes in it, and immediately turn them over to coat them with the hot oil. Sprinkle lightly with salt, then roast, turning once or twice, for the time given on the left:

CRISPY SAUTÉED POTATOES

SERVES 4 | SERVE HOT OFF THE PAN

2lb/900g potatoes, scrubbed

salt

2 tbsp flavorless oil such as sunflower or light olive oil

4 tbsp/2oz/50g butter or margarine

black pepper

Cook the potatoes whole in boiling salted water for 25–40 minutes, depending on size. Drain and return to the empty saucepan to dry over low heat, then cool, skin, and cut into thick slices or cubes.

To fry, put the oil and butter or margarine in a large heavy frying pan. When it starts to foam, add the potatoes and cook very gently for 15 minutes, shaking the pan occasionally so that they absorb the oil rather than fry in it. Increase the heat to make them crisp. Transfer them to a dish, leaving any excess oil behind, sprinkle with salt and pepper, and serve.

OVEN-CRISP POTATOES

SERVES 6
PARTLY COOKED POTATOES KEEP FOR 1 DAY IN THE FRIDGE | DO NOT FREEZE

2¼lb/1kg potatoes, scrubbed

1 tsp salt

4 tbsp/2oz/50g butter or margarine mixed with 2 tbsp sunflower oil, or ⅓ cup/100 ml sunflower or vegetable oil

2 onions, chopped if you are cubing your potatoes, or sliced if you are slicing your potatoes

TO SERVE

a little sea salt

10 grinds of black pepper

1 tbsp chopped parsley

Boil the potatoes in water and the salt for 25–40 minutes until tender. Drain and return to the empty saucepan to dry over low heat, then cool, skin, if you wish, and cut into ½in/1cm slices or cubes.

Heat the oil in a frying pan until the warmth can be felt on your hand held 2in/5cm above it. Add the onions and potatoes and cook gently for 10 minutes, stirring, until soft and golden. They should slowly absorb the oil rather than fry in it. Transfer to an oven tray wide enough to hold them in one layer—a 14 x 10 x 2in/35 x 25 x 5cm jelly roll pan is ideal.

Forty minutes before serving, put the dish in an oven preheated to 425°F/220°C for 30–40 minutes until crisp and golden, shaking occasionally. (The potatoes can be kept hot for up to 20 minutes at 350°F/180°C.)

Transfer to a serving dish, season with salt and black pepper, and toss with the parsley. Serve piping hot.

BREADS, BAKES, AND DESSERTS

RYE AND CARAWAY BREAD

MAKES 3 MEDIUM LOAVES
STAYS MOIST FOR 4–5 DAYS LOOSELY WRAPPED IN A PLASTIC BAG
FREEZES FOR 3 MONTHS

I am often asked for a recipe for a "real, old-fashioned rye bread." But which one, since there are literally dozens that qualify for that description? I chose this one because the method is simpler than most, yet the result is a light, moist, delicious loaf. Including beer gives the bread the traditional, tangy taste without the complexities of using a sourdough starter. Most of the preparation for the bread is done the day before baking, so you may need to plan ahead. Potato flour is available in kosher supermarkets, health food stores, and stores specializing in Eastern European ingredients.

4 tsp/½oz/14g instant yeast or ½ cake/1oz/25g fresh yeast

1 tbsp soft light brown sugar

4 cups/1¼lb/575g all-purpose flour, plus extra for dusting

3 cups/12oz/350g rye flour

3 tsp salt

3 tsp caraway seeds

2 cups/425ml beer

⅔ cup/150ml warm water

oil, for greasing

FOR THE GLAZE

1 tsp hot water and 1 tsp brown sugar, or 1 tsp potato flour and 2 tsp cold water

⅓ cup/85ml boiling water

With instant yeast, fit the dough hook in your electric mixer (use a mixer rather than a food processor, if possible), and mix together the yeast, brown sugar, both flours, salt, and 2 teaspoons of the caraway seeds. Add the beer and warm water and mix to a dough.

With fresh yeast, crumble the yeast into the bowl of your mixer, add the warm water and brown sugar, stir well, and set aside for 10 minutes, or until frothy. Add the beer to the yeast mixture, then, using the K beater of your electric mixer, add the well-mixed flours, salt, and 2 teaspoons of the caraway seeds, a cupful at a time, until the dough becomes too thick to continue. Change to the dough hook and add the remaining flour, mixing until it forms a dough.

Knead for 3–4 minutes until the dough has a silky, rather limp texture. Turn out on to a lightly floured surface, knead gently into a ball, then put in a well-oiled container large enough to let it expand to 3 times its size. Turn it over to make sure it is lightly coated with oil, cover with a lid or plastic wrap, and refrigerate overnight.

Continued on page 138

The following day, leave the dough (still in the container) in the warm kitchen for 1 1/2 hours until it has lost its chill (or warm on defrost in the microwave for 1 minute), then turn it out on to a floured surface and knead gently but firmly to expel all the gas bubbles.

Divide into three 1 lb/450g pieces. Knead each piece into a round or baton and arrange well apart on greased baking trays.

To make the glaze, either mix the hot water and sugar until dissolved, or mix the potato flour and cold water to a smooth, lump-free paste, then gradually whisk the boiling water into either mixture until you have a thick, clear paste.

Brush the loaves with your chosen glaze (reserving some if you are using potato flour), scatter with the remaining caraway seeds, and make 2 slanting slashes in the top with a sharp, floured knife. Slip each tray into a large plastic bag and leave until they have almost doubled in size and feel spongy to the touch—this will take about an 1 hour in a warm kitchen.

Meanwhile, preheat the oven to 400°F/200°C. Bake the loaves for 35–40 minutes, or until they are a deep chestnut color. If you are using the potato flour to glaze, brush the loaves again 15 minutes before the end of the baking time. Leave on a cooling rack until cool.

BAGELS

MAKES 15 BAGELS | PICTURED ON PAGE 142

Once you know that they must be boiled before they are baked, it is surprisingly easy to produce professional-looking bagels at home. Since you can make 15 bagels from just over 13oz/375g flour, it is worthwhile making a batch for the freezer, particularly if you live a long way from a source of good, authentic bagels.

The dough This is identical to the dough used for challah (see page 140), with the exception of the flour. Since bagels are much firmer in texture than bread, use about 2 tablespoons more flour than in the challah recipe— 13oz/375g of flour, instead of 12oz/350g, and skip the glaze (but you can still use sesame or poppy seeds, if desired).

Mix and refrigerate the dough for 9–12 hours or overnight in exactly the same way as for challah. The difference in technique starts once the risen dough is taken from the fridge.

To shape the bagels, work with the chilled dough direct from the fridge. Divide the dough into 15 pieces. Form each piece into a ball, then flatten with the palm of the hand and roll into a rope 7in/18cm long and ½in/1cm thick. Wind the rope around the knuckles of your hand. Press it on your work surface to seal the joint, then roll it gently back and forth to seal it firmly. Slip the bagel off your knuckles onto a floured board. Repeat with all the pieces of dough.

Leave to rise for 1 hour, until the bagels have increased slightly in size but are not as puffy as rolls. Preheat the oven to maximum (ideally 500°F/250°C) and have a very large pan of boiling water ready on the stove.

Put 5 or 6 bagels at a time into the boiling water and boil for 2 minutes, turning them over with a slotted spoon as they rise to the top. Drain from the water and lay on a cooling rack set over a board. Repeat with the remaining bagels. If you wish, dip the boiled bagels into a bowl of poppy or sesame seeds to coat.

Put the bagels on a floured baking sheet and bake in the hot oven for 1 minute to dry the top surface, then flip and bake for a further 15 minutes until they are a rich, shiny brown.

CHALLAH

MAKES 1 LARGE BRAIDED LOAF, 12–15IN/30–38CM LONG OR
1 MEDIUM PAN LOAF | PICTURED ON PAGE 143
KEEPS FOR 3–4 DAYS AT ROOM TEMPERATURE IN A BREAD CONTAINER
FREEZES FOR 3 MONTHS BAKED, OR FOR 2 WEEKS SHAPED AND READY FOR BAKING

This is best made in a mixer rather than a food processor.

2 tsp/¼oz/7g instant yeast or
¼ cake/½oz/14g fresh yeast

2½ cups/12oz/350g all-purpose
flour, plus extra for dusting

¾ tsp salt

2 tbsp/1oz/25g sugar or 1 rounded
tbsp honey (this can be reduced to
1 tbsp if preferred)

⅔ cup/150ml warm water

2 tbsp sunflower or other
flavorless oil

1 large egg

FOR THE GLAZE

1 egg yolk

1 tsp water

1 good pinch of salt

poppyseeds or sesame seeds

If using instant yeast, mix the yeast thoroughly with the other dry ingredients, then add all the remaining ingredients to the bowl.

If using fresh yeast, attach the dough hook to your mixer, then put the water into the mixing bowl, followed by a third of the flour, the crumbled yeast, and the sugar or honey. Mix until smooth—about 2 minutes—then cover with a dish towel and leave for 10–15 minutes until it has frothed up. Add all the remaining ingredients for the dough.

Now mix at low speed until a sticky ball begins to form, then turn to medium speed, and knead for 4–5 minutes until the dough is slapping against the edges of the bowl, leaving it clean as it goes around. If it still looks very sticky, work in a further 1–2 tablespoons of flour; if dry, add water a teaspoon at a time until the dough reaches the right consistency.

Tip the dough onto a floured board and knead with your hands for a further minute until it is tight and springy with a silky feel—as smooth as a baby's cheek! Grease a large bowl with oil, turn the dough in it to coat all sides with oil (this stops the surface drying out), cover with plastic wrap, and leave to rise in the fridge. If it rises before you have time to deal with it (it takes 9–12 hours but can be left for up to 24 hours), punch it down and leave it to rise again.

To shape the loaves, take the risen dough from the fridge and leave it to come to room temperature in the kitchen—about 1 hour. Or put it in the microwave on the defrost setting for 1½–2 minutes until warm to the touch.

Divide the dough in half and work on each half as follows. Knead the dough by hand or machine to break down any large bubbles of gas, then leave for 5 minutes with a cloth to "relax."

To make a 3-strand braid, divide the piece of dough into 3. Flatten each piece with a fist, then roll up into a little Swiss roll. Flatten again, roll up as before, then shape into a ball—this greatly improves the texture of the loaf.

Roll each ball into a 12in/30cm strand that tapers slightly at each end. Join the 3 strands firmly together at one end, then fan them out on the board. Braid in the usual way. Arrange on a greased tray.

To make a pan loaf, lightly grease a 2lb/900g loaf pan measuring about about 9 x 5 x 3in/22.5 x 12.5 x 7.5cm. Divide the remaining dough into 3 and flatten each piece with your fist, then roll up into a little Swiss roll, flatten, roll up again, then finally roll into a ball. Arrange 2 of the balls side by side in the center of the pan. Divide the third ball in half, then shape it into two smaller balls and place these on either side of the center balls. Brush with the glaze and scatter with poppy or sesame seeds.

To proof either the braid or the loaf, slip the tray or the loaf pan into a large plastic bag. This creates a miniature "greenhouse" atmosphere—damp and free from draughts—which the dough needs to rise. Leave in a warm place for 45 minutes to 1 hour, or until puffy again. Remove from the bag.

To bake the bread, preheat the oven to 450°F/230°C. Put the bread in the oven and immediately turn the temperature down to 400°F/200°C. Bake the braid for 25–30 minutes or until crusty and brown; bake the loaf for 30–40 minutes, or until the bottom sounds hollow when tapped.

GERMAN BUTTER KUCHEN
WITH DATE FILLING

**MAKES 1 LARGE LOAF | KEEPS FRESH FOR 2 DAYS IN THE FRIDGE
COOKED KUCHEN FREEZES FOR 3 MONTHS; UNRISEN DOUGH FOR 3 MONTHS;
SHAPED BUT UNCOOKED KUCHEN FOR 2 WEEKS**

This butter cake is delicious when sliced and spread with butter or cream cheese. It is also good toasted, once it begins to dry out after a few days.

1 quantity risen kuchen dough (see page 182)

a little flour, for dusting

FOR THE DATE FILLING

1 ½ cups/8oz/225g pitted dried dates, chopped

1 tbsp/½oz/15g butter or margarine

1 ½ tsp ground cinnamon

¼ cup/1½oz/40g golden raisins

FOR THE ICING

⅓ cup/2oz/50g sifted confectioner's sugar

about 2 tsp lemon or orange juice

¼ cup/1oz/25g chopped walnuts

FOR THE CINNAMON RAISIN FILLING

2 tbsp butter

¼ cup/2oz/50g soft light brown sugar

1 tsp ground cinnamon

⅓ cup/2oz/50g raisins

To make the filling, put all the ingredients into a pan, cover, and simmer, stirring occasionally, until the mixture forms a thick, juicy paste. Allow to cool.

Grease a 2lb/900g loaf pan measuring about 9 x 5 x 3in/23 x 13 x 7.5cm. Roll out the dough on a lightly floured board into a rectangle 1in/2.5cm wider than the base of the loaf pan and ½in/1cm thick. Spread with the filling to within ½in/1cm of either side, then turn these sides over the filling to seal it in, and roll up tightly into a Swiss roll. Lay it in the pan, join-side down. Put the pan into a large plastic bag and leave in a warm place until the kuchen looks puffy and feels spongy to the touch, about 30–40 minutes.

Meanwhile, preheat the oven to 350°F/180°C. Bake the kuchen for 35–40 minutes until golden brown and firm to a gentle touch. Make the icing by adding just enough fruit juice to the confectioner's sugar to make a thick coating consistency. Turn the baked kuchen out onto a cooling rack and, while still warm, spread with the icing and decorate with the nuts.

VARIATION
CINNAMON RAISIN FILLING
Mix all the ingredients (left) together until spreadable. Use to fill the kuchen as above.

FRUITED KUCHEN RING

MAKES A 9IN/23CM CAKE

½ quantity risen kuchen dough
(see page 182)

FOR THE FILLING

¼ cup/2oz/50g sugar

1 tsp cinnamon

2 tbsp/1oz/30g melted butter

⅓ cup/2oz/50g raisins

FOR THE GLAZE

1 tbsp lemon juice

⅔ cup/3oz/75g confectioner's
sugar

Roll the dough into a rectangle about 12in/28cm by 6in/15cm. Combine the filling ingredients then spread in an even layer over the dough. Starting at the long side nearest to you, roll up into a tight roll, then join the ends together to form a ring. Line a baking tray with parchment paper and transfer the ring to it. Using kitchen scissors, make cuts two-thirds of the way through the dough at 1½in/4cm intervals to reveal some of the filling. Slip the tray into a large plastic bag and leave to rise in a warm place until puffy—this should take about 30 minutes. Preheat the oven to 400°F/200°C. Bake the ring for 25 minutes. Beat the glaze ingredients together until smooth then drizzle over the warm kuchen.

SCHNECKEN
GERMAN SWEET BUNS

MAKES 12
KEEPS FOR 2 DAYS IN THE FRIDGE | FREEZES FOR 3 MONTHS

½ quantity risen kuchen dough
(see page 182)

FOR THE GLAZE

2 tbsp/1oz/30g butter, plus more
for greasing the pan

2 tbsp brown sugar

2 tbsp golden syrup or honey

FOR THE FILLING

2 tbsp/1oz/30g soft butter

¼ cup/2oz/50g sugar

1 tsp ground cinnamon

⅓ cup /2oz/50g raisins

¼ cup/1oz/25g chopped walnuts

Grease a 12-hole muffin pan. Simmer the glaze ingredients in a pan for 1 minute, or until a rich golden brown. Divide between the holes of the pan.

For the filling, put the butter in a bowl and beat in the sugar and cinnamon, then the raisins and walnuts. Roll out the dough on a lightly floured board to ½in/1cm thick, in a rectangle 12 x 6in/ 30 x 15cm. Spread with the filling. Roll up lengthways into a tight roll, then cut into 1in/2.5cm slices. Arrange these, cut-side up, in the muffin pan. Slip the tray into a plastic bag and leave until puffy—30–40 minutes. Meanwhile, preheat the oven to 400°F/200°C. Bake the buns for 15–20 minutes, or until a rich brown. Allow 5 minutes for the glaze to set a little, then remove the schnecken from the pan and leave them, with the glaze on top, on a cooling rack.

TRADITIONAL CHEESECAKE

SERVES 10

KEEPS FOR 3 DAYS IN THE FRIDGE | FREEZES FOR 2 MONTHS

This is an updated version of the traditional cheesecake from Eastern Europe that used to be made with homemade kaese (curd cheese) and baked in a pie crust. It is rather more luxurious than older recipes, but since most of us make this cake only on special occasions, I think it is worth putting in the finest ingredients and making it in a size to serve a crowd.

1 recipe quantity cheesecake pastry crust (see page 183)

FOR THE FILLING

3 eggs, separated

1 pinch of salt

1 1/2 cups/12oz/350g low- or medium-fat cream cheese

1/2 cup/2oz/50g ground almonds

2 tbsp/1oz/25g soft butter

1/2 cup/2oz/50g superfine sugar

3 tbsp lemon juice

grated zest of 1/2 lemon

1/2 tsp vanilla extract

1/3 cup/2oz/60g golden raisins

FOR DECORATION

1 tbsp sugar

1/4 cup/1oz/25g sliced almonds

Preheat the oven to 350°F/180°C.

Put the egg yolks and whites in separate mixing bowls. Add the salt to the egg whites and whisk until they hold floppy peaks. Add all the remaining ingredients except the raisins to the egg yolks and mix until thoroughly blended. Carefully fold the egg whites into the cheese mixture. Stir in the raisins, then pour into the unbaked pastry base.

Take the egg white leftover from making the pastry and whisk until frothy. Paint it over the cheese mixture, then sprinkle with the granulated sugar. Scatter with the almonds.

Bake the larger cheesecake for 40 minutes, and the smaller, deeper cheesecake for 20 minutes, then turn the oven down to 325°F/160°C and bake for a further 30 minutes. In either case, the cheesecake is ready when it is a pale gold color and firm to gentle touch around the edges. (The filling continues to set as it cools.) Loosen the edges with a knife as soon as possible to help prevent cracking.

LUSCIOUS LEMON CAKE

MAKES A 6IN/15CM SQUARE CAKE
KEEPS FOR 1 WEEK IN AN AIRTIGHT CONTAINER AT ROOM TEMPERATURE
FREEZES FOR 3 MONTHS

This delicate sponge cake, moistened with a tart lemon syrup, must be my all-time family favorite and is the star of a thousand bake sales. The cake will stay moist for as long as as any of it remains uneaten!

1 stick/4oz/125g soft butter or margarine

scant 1 cup/6oz/175g superfine sugar

2/3 cup/3oz/85g all-purpose flour

2/3 cup/3oz/85g cake flour

1 tsp baking powder

1/3 cup/80ml milk

zest of 1 lemon

2 large eggs, beaten

pinch of salt

FOR THE SYRUP

2/3 cup/3oz/75g confectioner's sugar, plus extra for dusting

Juice of 1 1/2 large lemons

Preheat the oven to 350°F/180°C. Grease a 15cm/6in square cake pan and line the bottom with parchment paper—this is important. (Alternatively, grease and line a 2lb/900g loaf pan, 9 x 5 x 3in/ 22.5 x 12.5 x 7.5cm).

Put all the cake ingredients into a bowl and beat with a mixer or wooden spoon until smooth—about 3 minutes. Pour the cake mixture into the pan and smooth the top with the back of a spoon. Bake for 45 minutes.

Remove from the oven and place the cake, still in the pan, on a cooling rack. Gently heat the sugar and lemon juice just until a clear syrup is formed. Prick the warm cake all over with a fork, then gently pour the syrup over it, spooning it from the sides until it has been completely absorbed.

Leave until the cake is cool, then carefully turn out. Serve, dusted with confectioner's sugar.

LITHUANIAN CHOCOLATE AND NUT TORTE

MAKES A 8IN/20CM CAKE
KEEPS FOR 1 WEEK IN AN AIRTIGHT CONTAINER IN THE FRIDGE
FREEZES FOR 3 MONTHS

This kind of flourless chocolate cake is made all over the Baltic States and the countries of the former Austro-Hungarian Empire. It is moist yet light in texture, worthy of a special occasion.

1 cup/4oz/100g ground almonds

3 tbsp fine dried breadcrumbs

4oz/100g good-quality dark chocolate, grated

3 large eggs, separated

heaped ½ cup/4½oz/125g superfine sugar

1 tbsp lemon juice

FOR THE COATING

1 tbsp strong coffee or 2 tsp instant coffee dissolved in 1 tbsp hot water

1 tbsp Tia Maria or similar coffee liqueur

3 tbsp hot chocolate mix

6 tbsp/3oz/75g butter, softened

½ cup/3oz/75g confectioner's sugar

TO SERVE

8 whole blanched almonds, toasted in a dry pan

Preheat the oven to 350°F/180°C. Have ready a 8in/20cm round loose-bottomed cake pan, greased and lined with parchment paper.

Mix the ground almonds, crumbs, and the grated chocolate. Whisk the egg whites until they hold stiff peaks, then add the sugar, a tablespoon at a time, whisking until stiff after each addition. Fold in the egg yolks, followed by the dry ingredients. Finally, stir in the lemon juice. Spoon the mixture into the prepared pan and level the top.

Bake for 45 minutes until golden brown and firm to a gentle touch—a skewer inserted in the center should come out clean. Leave on a cooling rack until cold, then carefully turn out.

To make the icing, put the coffee, liqueur, and hot chocolate mix in a bowl and mix well. Stir in the butter and confectioner's sugar and beat until smooth. Coat the cake all over with the icing and decorate with toasted almonds.

APPLE KUCHEN

MAKES A 4¹/₂ X 3¹/₂IN/12 X 9CM STREUSEL
MAKE AND EAT THE SAME DAY

This is delicious served hot or cold. A layer of thinly sliced apple is baked on the kuchen batter. It is best eaten the same day.

1 quantity quick kuchen batter (see page 183)

1 lb 5oz/600g cooking apples

FOR THE TOPPING (OPTIONAL)

¹/₃ cup/2oz/50g all-purpose flour

2 tsp ground cinnamon

scant 1 cup/5oz/150g light brown sugar

4 tbsp/2oz/60g butter

Preheat the oven to 375°F/190°C.

If using, make the topping. Mix together the flour, cinnamon, and sugar. Melt the butter, then pour onto the dry ingredients and blend with a fork until evenly moistened.

Evenly spread the kuchen dough in a greased baking pan measuring 12 x 9 x 2in/30 x 23 x 4cm.

Peel, core, and quarter the apples, then cut them into thin slices ¹/₈in/3mm thick. Arrange the apple slices in overlapping rows so that the kuchen batter is completely covered. Sprinkle the topping over the apples.

Bake for 30–40 minutes, or until the cake has shrunk from the sides of the pan, the apples feel tender when pierced with a knife, and the top is golden brown.

DUTCH APPLE SPONGE CAKE

MAKES 12 GOOD-SIZED SQUARES
KEEPS FOR 2 DAYS IN THE FRIDGE | FREEZES FOR 3 MONTHS

On a cold winter's night, how good it is to come home to a nice, comforting hot dessert! And it doesn't have to be unhealthy, either. With lots of fruit, unrefined sugar, and wholewheat flour, it can be nutritious as well as warming and delicious. Although best served hot, if there is any leftover, this doubles as a very respectable apple cake.

scant 2 cups/9oz/250g
all-purpose or wholewheat flour

3 tsp baking powder

½ cup/4oz/125g light brown sugar

3 eggs

6 tbsp/3oz/75g soft margarine

1 tsp grated lemon zest

FOR THE TOPPING

2lb/900g large tart eating apples
such as Braeburn

2½ tbsp lemon juice

4 tbsp/2oz/50g butter, melted

½ cup/4oz/125g soft
brown sugar

1½ tsp ground cinnamon

TO SERVE

whipped cream, ice cream, or Greek
yogurt drizzled with honey

Preheat the oven to 400°F/200°C. Grease a shallow cake pan about 12 x 8in/30 x 20cm.

Place all the cake ingredients in a bowl with ½ cup/ 125ml water and mix until smooth—3 minutes by hand, 2 minutes by electric mixer, 20 seconds by food processor, scraping down the sides halfway with a rubber spatula. Spoon into the pan and smooth the top level with a knife.

Peel, core, and slice the apples ⅛in/3mm thick. Toss the slices in a bowl with the lemon juice, then arrange in tightly packed, overlapping rows on top of the cake mixture, covering it completely. Drizzle the melted butter on top, mix the sugar and cinnamon, and sprinkle this evenly over the apples.

Bake for around 45 minutes until the cake is a rich brown and the apples are tender. Serve warm or at room temperature with whipped cream, ice cream, or Greek yogurt drizzled with honey.

APPLE CRISP

SERVES 6

KEEPS FOR 3 DAYS IN THE FRIDGE | FREEZES FOR 3 MONTHS

This recipe is simple to make, uncomplicated in flavor, and utterly delicious to eat. It works equally well with pitted plums, or a combination of plums and apples.

4 large cooking apples
(or a mixture of Macintosh and
Granny Smith apples)

¼ cup/2oz/50g brown sugar mixed
with ½ tsp ground cinnamon

1 tbsp lemon juice

FOR THE TOPPING

generous ½ cup/3oz/75g
all-purpose flour

3 tbsp rolled oats

½ cup/4oz/125g soft brown sugar

6 tbsp/3oz/75g margarine or butter

TO SERVE

custard, ice cream, or yogurt
(optional)

Preheat the oven to 375°F/190°C. Peel, core, and slice the apples into a shallow baking or gratin dish approximately 11 x 8 x 1½in/ 28 x 20 x 4cm deep. Sprinkle them with the mixed sugar and cinnamon, followed by the lemon juice and ⅓ cup/75ml water.

For the topping, combine the flour, oats, and brown sugar, then gently rub in the butter or margarine until the mixture is crumbly. Sprinkle in an even layer over the apples.

Bake for 1 hour, or until crunchy and golden brown. Serve plain or with custard, ice cream, or yogurt.

FAYE'S NEW-STYLE LOKSHEN KUGEL

SERVES 6

LEFTOVERS KEEP FOR 3 DAYS IN THE FRIDGE | FREEZE FOR 3 MONTHS

This is a fruitier version of the traditional noodle pudding, sweetened by a little honey instead of a lot of sugar. It does not have the crustiness of the original but is altogether lighter in texture.

1 ½ cups/8oz/225g dried broad egg noodles

2 eating apples

½ cup/4oz/125g candied cherries

4 tbsp/2oz/50g margarine or butter

¾ cup/4oz/125g golden raisins

¾ cup/4oz/125g raisins

1 egg

1 tsp ground allspice

2 ½ tbsp orange juice

1 rounded tbsp mild-tasting honey

TO SERVE

fresh strawberries (optional)

Break the noodles into pieces and boil until tender according to the package instructions.

Peel, core, and grate the apples. Wash and slice the cherries. Melt the butter or margarine.

Preheat the oven to 300°F/150°C. Mix all the ingredients gently but firmly together, then turn into a greased 5 cup/1.2l soufflé dish. Cover with foil and bake for 1 ½ hours. Turn out onto a plate and serve plain or with fresh strawberries.

MIRKATAN

ARMENIAN FRUIT COMPÔTE

SERVES 6
KEEPS FOR 4 DAYS IN THE FRIDGE | DO NOT FREEZE

In this ancient Armenian recipe, plump and juicy dried fruits mixed with nuts and orange segments are macerated in a delicately spiced wine syrup. The compôte can be served either warm or cold, plain or accompanied in the traditional manner by rosewater-scented whipped cream, or, as I prefer it, with Greek yogurt lightly sweetened with Hymettus honey.

I cup/6oz/175g pitted prunes

I cup/6oz/175g dried apricots

I cup/6oz/175g dried peaches or pears

enough freshly brewed tea to cover the dried fruit

¼ cup/2oz/50g walnut halves

scant ½ cup/100 ml fruity red wine

3 strips of orange rind

I cinnamon stick

¼ cup/2oz/50g superfine sugar

I tbsp fresh lemon juice

I tbsp orange blossom water

2 navel oranges, peeled and sectioned

TO SERVE (OPTIONAL)

whipped cream with a few drops of rosewater mixed in, or Greek yogurt drizzled with honey

The day before, put the dried fruits in a bowl and pour the strained tea over it. Cover and leave overnight.

The next day, strain the fruit into a bowl, reserving the liquid, and insert the walnut halves into the prunes. If necessary, add enough water to the reserved tea to make a scant I cup/200 ml. Pour this into a wide pan with the wine, orange rind, cinnamon stick, and sugar. Bring to a boil and simmer, uncovered, for 3 minutes.

Add the dried fruit, cover, and simmer for 20 minutes until the fruit is tender and the syrup has thickened. Stir in the lemon juice, orange blossom water, and orange sections. Serve hot or cold, either plain or with your choice of topping.

TRADITIONAL KICHELS

MAKES ABOUT 50, DEPENDING ON SIZE
KEEP FOR 2 WEEKS IN AN AIRTIGHT CONTAINER | FREEZE FOR 3 MONTHS

These orange and vanilla cookies are a favorite for all kinds of occasions because they do not include any dairy products and so are suitable to serve before, with, or after either a meat or a dairy meal. Use only the minimum amount of flour needed to achieve a rollable dough, and the kichels will be light and crisp.

generous 1 cup/5oz/150g cake flour

1–1½ cups/5–7oz/150-200g all-purpose flour

3 tsp baking powder

2 large eggs

⅔ cup/5oz/150g superfine sugar, plus extra for sprinkling

½ cup/125ml sunflower or other flavorless oil

zest of 1 orange

1 tsp vanilla extract

Preheat the oven to 350°F/180°C and line 2 baking sheets with parchment paper.

Mix the flours and baking powder. In a separate bowl, whisk the eggs until thick, then gradually whisk in the sugar, followed by the oil, orange zest, and vanilla. Finally stir in enough of the flour to make a rollable, nonsticky dough. Knead until smooth, then roll out on a floured board until ½in/1 cm thick.

Sprinkle the dough with sugar, then roll lightly to press it in. Cut into shapes with cookie cutters and arrange on the prepared trays, leaving room for the cookies to spread. Bake for 20–25 minutes, or until a pale gold in color. Leave on wire racks until cooled.

JUDEBROD
DANISH CARDAMOM COOKIES

MAKES ABOUT 60
KEEP FOR 1 WEEK IN AN AIRTIGHT CONTAINER | FREEZE FOR 6 WEEKS

Cardamom—that wonderfully aromatic spice that gives authentic Danish pastries their unique flavor—magically transforms these quickly made, melt-in-the-mouth cookies into very special petits fours to serve with a compôte of summer fruits or ice cream.

1 stick/4oz/120g butter, cut into roughly 1 in/2.5cm chunks

½ cup/4oz/125g light muscovado or light brown sugar

1 tsp ground cinnamon

1 tsp freshly pounded cardamom seeds or ground cardamom

1 egg

1 tsp baking powder

scant 1 cup/4½oz/130g all-purpose flour

1 cup/4½oz/130g cake flour

FOR THE DECORATION

2 tbsp brown or white sanding sugar

¼ cup/1oz/25g sliced almonds

If you're making them by hand, work all the ingredients together until a dough is formed.

To use a food processor, put all the ingredients in the bowl of your machine and process or pulse just until little moist balls of dough begin to form. Tip into a bowl and knead into a dough.

Flatten into a block 1 in/2.5cm thick, then chill for several hours or overnight.

Preheat the oven to 375°F/190°C and grease or line baking sheets with parchment paper. Mix the sanding sugar and sliced almonds together.

Roll out the dough ⅛in/3mm thick and stamp out 2in/5cm rounds with a cookie cutter. Brush the circles lightly with water, then dip them into the sugar and almond mixture (or sprinkle this mixture on top).

Place the cookies on the prepared baking sheets and bake for 10–12 minutes, or until firm to the touch. Leave on wire racks until cool.

GEREYBES
SEPHARDI SHORTBREAD "BRACELETS"

MAKES ABOUT 36
KEEP FOR 2 WEEKS IN AN AIRTIGHT CONTAINER AT ROOM TEMPERATURE
FREEZE FOR 3 MONTHS

The baking of the Sephardim, particularly those from communities in the Middle East, is of a delicacy and refinement rarely equaled in Western cooking. Craft plays a great part in shaping the many different kinds of pastries of which this delicate butter cookie is typical. This recipe comes from a family with roots in Damascus in the late 19th century.

2 sticks/8oz/225g unsalted butter, at room temperature

²/₃ cup/5oz/150g superfine sugar

1 ¼ cup/6oz/175g all-purpose flour, mixed with 1 ⅓ cup/6oz/175g cake flour, plus more for dusting

½ cup/2oz/50g split blanched almonds

Preheat the oven to 325°F/160°C.

Using an electric mixer, cream the butter until it is the texture of mayonnaise, then gradually add the sugar, beating until the mixture is almost white. Add the flour mixture, a little at a time, beating after each addition. When enough flour has been added, the dough should come away from the edges of the bowl.

Turn out onto a lightly floured board and knead gently but thoroughly until the dough is quite smooth. Take a piece of the dough and roll into a salami shape about 1in/2.5cm in diameter, then cut across at ½in/1cm intervals into short pieces. Roll each of these in turn into a pencil shape about 5in/13cm long. Form into a small "bracelet" by slightly overlapping the ends, then put a split almond over the join. Repeat with the remaining dough.

Arrange on ungreased baking trays leaving 1in/2.5cm between each cookie. Bake for 18–20 minutes, or until the cookies are barely colored and just firm to the touch—do not overbrown or the delicate flavor will be compromised. Leave on the trays until cold. Store in an airtight container.

APPLE BUWELE
PASTRY-WRAPPED APPLE

SERVES 6
KEEPS FOR 3 DAYS IN THE FRIDGE | FREEZES UNTIL REQUIRED

Wrapped in tender yeast dough, a cinnamon-scented apple filling is the heart of a famous South German–Jewish dish traditionally served at Sukkot.

FOR THE YEAST PASTRY

3½ cups/1 lb/450g all-purpose flour, plus extra for dusting

½ tsp salt

2 tsp/¼oz/7g instant yeast

⅓ cup/3oz/75g sugar

2 eggs

⅔ cup/150ml warm milk or water

6 tbsp/3 oz/75g soft butter or margarine or ½ cup/125ml oil, plus more for greasing

FOR THE APPLE FILLING

1½lb/675g cooking apples

2 tbsp/1oz/25g butter or margarine

⅓ cup/3oz/75g soft light brown sugar

1 tbsp lemon juice

3 tbsp raisins or golden raisins

FOR THE TOPPING

¾ cup/3oz/75g confectioner's sugar

1 tbsp lemon juice

a few sliced almonds

To make the pastry, mix the flour, salt, yeast, and sugar in a bowl. Put the eggs in a measuring jug and make up to about 1 cup/250ml with the milk or water, whisking well. Add to the dry ingredients with the soft butter or oil, and mix with a beater or dough hook for about 5 minutes until it forms a soft, shiny ball that leaves the sides of the bowl clean. If it is too soft, add a little more flour. Turn onto a floured board, knead for 30 seconds, then put into an oiled bowl and turn it over to coat it well. Cover with plastic wrap. It can now be given 3–4 bursts of 50 percent power (500W) for 20 seconds each, at 5-minute intervals, in the microwave. This will almost halve the rising time. Otherwise, leave it in a warm place until double in bulk—about 1½ hours. Knead it for 1–2 minutes, then set aside again for 10 minutes.

While the dough is rising the first time, prepare the filling: peel, core, and thinly slice the apples, then put them into a sauté pan with all the remaining ingredients and cook gently until soft but not mushy. Allow to cool until quite cold.

To shape the strudel, roll the dough into a large rectangle about ½in/1 cm thick, spread with the filling, turn in the sides, and roll up gently, starting from a long edge. Lay on a greased baking tray and bend into a horseshoe. Put the whole tray into a large plastic bag and leave until puffy—about 30 minutes. Preheat the oven to 400°F/200°C. Remove the tray from the bag and bake for 35–40 minutes until a rich brown. Cool for 5 minutes, then brush with icing made by mixing the sugar and juice until smooth. Sprinkle with the almonds, then leave to cool and set.

VANILLA KIPFERL

MAKES 18

KEEP FOR 2 WEEKS AT ROOM TEMPERATURE IN AN AIRTIGHT CONTAINER | FREEZE FOR 3 MONTHS

The pride and joy of every Jewish cook of Austro-Hungarian origin, the kipferl is one of the great cookies of the world. It has been served in the konditorei (coffee houses) of Vienna and Budapest since the 17th century. The cookies can be made by hand, like shortbread, or in a processor or mixer, but in the latter case take care not to overmix the sugar and butter.

½ cup/2½oz/70g all-purpose flour

½ cup/2½oz/70g cake flour

1 pinch of salt

¼ cup/1oz/25g ground almonds or hazelnuts, or a mixture of both

1 stick/4oz/100g butter at room temperature, cut into 1in/2.5cm chunks

2 tbsp superfine sugar

1 tbsp vanilla sugar

1 egg yolk

sifted confectioner's sugar, for coating

To make the cookies using the traditional method, put the flours, salt, and nuts on a board, make a well in the center, and add the butter, sugar, and vanilla sugar. Work these together with your fingers, blend in the egg yolk, then gradually work in the surrounding dry ingredients until a dough is formed.

Alternatively, in a mixer, work the butter, sugar, and vanilla sugar together until absorbed. Mix in the egg yolk. Gradually add the flours, ground nuts, and salt until the dough leaves the side of the bowl clean.

Chill for 1 hour. Preheat the oven to 325°F/160°C. In shaping the cookies, do not use any flour on your work surface because this will toughen them. A marble or granite surface is ideal, or you can use a silicone baking mat. Pinch off pieces of dough the size of a walnut and roll between your palms into 36 smooth, even balls. Roll each ball under your hand into a "pencil" about ½in/1cm thick and 3½–4in/9–10cm long, then bend into a crescent. Arrange on ungreased baking sheets, leaving about 1in/2.5cm between each cookie, since they do spread a little. Bake for 18 minutes, or until a very pale-gold color (they must not brown). Using a flat spatula, carefully lift the cookies onto a cooling rack and leave for 3 minutes to firm up, then dip into a bowl of confectioner's sugar. Dip again when completely cold. Allow to mature for 24 hours in an airtight container.

ALMOND MACAROONS

MAKES ABOUT 12
KEEP FOR 1 WEEK IN AN AIRTIGHT CONTAINER IN THE FRIDGE
FREEZE FOR 3 MONTHS

This is my definitive recipe after many years of failure or only partial success. The secret seems to lie in the amount of egg white used—just the right uncooked texture and the macaroons will bake crisp on the outside and be moist and chewy within.

1 ¼ cups/4oz/125g ground almonds

1 ½–2 egg whites (3–4 tbsp/ 40–50 ml) broken up with a fork

⅔ cup/5oz/150g superfine sugar

2 tbsp vanilla sugar

sifted confectioner's sugar

12–13 blanched almond halves (optional)

Preheat the oven to 400°F/200°C. Cover a baking tray with parchment paper.

Put the ground almonds into a food processor and process for 15 seconds, or until very fine.

Add about half an egg white, and process for another 10 seconds. Then add half the sugar and the vanilla sugar, and process for another 10 seconds. Add another half an egg white and the remaining sugar in the same way. Then add a further half egg white. The mixture will now be soft but just capable of being formed into balls with your hands. If it is too stiff, add the remaining egg white.

Take pieces of the dough and roll between your hands into balls the size of a large walnut—you should get 12 or 13 balls. If you make more, they're too small and should be re-rolled.

Put the balls 2in/5cm apart on the parchment paper and gently flatten with your fingers. Brush all over with cold water, then sprinkle with the confectioner's sugar. Place an almond half on each one, or leave plain, as you prefer.

Bake for 15– 17 minutes, or until the tops are just lightly browned. Over-baking will result in crisp instead of moist macaroons. Remove from the tray using a spatula. When cold, store in an airtight container.

CINNAMON BALLS

MAKES 20–22
KEEP FOR 1 WEEK IN AN AIRTIGHT CONTAINER AT ROOM TEMPERATURE
FREEZE FOR 3 MONTHS

This must be the definitive recipe for this famous Anglo-Jewish cookie—a crisp shell enclosing a soft, fudgy interior. The inside will stay soft and moist, provided the cinnamon balls are not overbaked. Delicious with tea or coffee, or as after-dinner petits fours.

2 egg whites

1/2 cup/4oz/125g superfine sugar

2 1/4 cups/8oz/225g ground almonds

1 tbsp ground cinnamon

sifted confectioner's sugar, for coating

Preheat the oven to 325°F/160°C and grease a baking sheet.

Beat the whites until they form stiff peaks. Gently stir in all the remaining ingredients, mixing until even in color. With wetted hands, form into 20–22 balls and arrange on the prepared baking sheet.

Bake for 18–20 minutes, or until just firm to the touch. Roll in confectioner's sugar while still warm and then again when cool.

VARIATION
CINNAMON AND WALNUT BALLS
Fold in 1/2 cup/2oz/50g finely chopped walnuts before forming the balls

BASICS

RICE AND GRAIN DISHES
COUSCOUS

SERVES 4

KEEPS FOR 2 DAYS IN THE FRIDGE | FREEZES FOR 3 MONTHS

Although fine-grain couscous looks similar to bulgar, couscous is actually a type of dried pasta. The "grains" are made by rolling moist semolina wheat, then coating them with fine flour. It is traditionally steamed, rather than boiled, to produce a wonderfully light, fluffy texture.

2 cups/12oz/350g couscous

¼ cup/60ml sunflower or olive oil

1 tsp salt

lukewarm water

Put the couscous and oil in a bowl and add the salt. Add lukewarm water to twice the depth of the couscous. Stir well for 1 minute, then drain in a sieve.

For a small quantity, leave in the sieve and steam, covered, over boiling water for 10 minutes until fluffy and separate.

For a larger quantity, line the top of the steamer with a light-colored non-woven kitchen cloth, add the drained couscous, cover, and steam for 10 minutes.

Alternatively, in the microwave, reheat, covered, on 100 percent (1000W) power for 1 – 1 ½ minutes.

SIMPLE RICE PILAF

SERVES 6
KEEPS FOR 3 DAYS IN THE FRIDGE | FREEZES FOR 3 MONTHS

This gives a rather more savory result than Turkish rice pilaf, below, but does involve sautéing both the onion and the rice. It works well for rice that will be served cold in salads.

1 ³/₄ cups/12oz/350g basmati rice

3 tbsp oil

1 onion, finely chopped

scant 3 cups/700ml hot chicken stock (see page 176)

2 tsp salt

15 grinds of black pepper

Rinse the rice in a sieve under cold water until the water runs clear. Heat the oil in a heavy-based saucepan and cook the onion for 5 minutes until soft and golden. Add the rice and turn in the onion and oil for 3 minutes. Stir in the hot stock, salt, and pepper. Bring to a boil, then cover tightly and cook over low heat for 20 minutes, either on the stovetop, or in the oven at 400°F/200°C. Fluff up the rice with a fork before serving.

TURKISH RICE PILAF

SERVES 6
KEEPS FOR 3 DAYS IN THE FRIDGE | FREEZES FOR 6 MONTHS

A superbly flavored dish to serve with roast chicken or lamb chops.

1 ³/₄ cups/10oz/275g basmati rice

1 heaped tbsp margarine

1 onion, finely chopped

2 ¹/₂ cups/575 ml hot chicken stock

¹/₄ tsp turmeric

¹/₂ tsp salt

¹/₄ tsp ground cinnamon

¹/₃ cup/2oz/50g golden raisins

¹/₃ cup/2oz/50g unsalted pistachios, blanched and halved, or
¹/₂ cup/2oz/50g cashews, dry toasted

Make in exactly the same way as the plain rice pilaf (above), adding all the spices and the raisins with the hot liquid. Stir in the nuts with a fork just before serving.

PERSIAN CHILAU RICE

SERVES 4 | PICTURED RIGHT
KEEPS FOR 2 DAYS IN THE FRIDGE | FREEZES FOR 3 MONTHS

1 cup/6oz/175g basmati rice

1 tbsp salt

1 ½ tbsp sunflower oil

3 cardamom pods

Cover the rice in cold water and soak for 30 minutes. Strain and rinse under cold running water until the water runs clear. Bring a large heavy saucepan of water to a boil with the salt. Add the rice and cook, uncovered, bubbling steadily, for 7 minutes, or until a grain feels almost tender when bitten. Turn into a sieve, rinse thoroughly under hot running water, then drain well. Put half of the oil and 1 tablespoon water into the pan and heat until it steams, then add half of the rice, the cardamom pods, and the remaining oil. Add the rest of the rice. Wrap a dish towel under the lid of the pan, then place it firmly into position. Leave on the lowest heat for 20 minutes. The result is perfect, fluffy rice. And the crunchy layer that forms on the base of the pan is particularly prized.

PERSIAN CHELLO RICE

SERVES 6
KEEPS FOR 3 DAYS IN THE FRIDGE | FREEZES FOR 3 MONTHS

1 ⅓ cups/11 oz/300g basmati rice

2 tbsp salt

¼ cup/60ml oil

Soak the rice in cold water for 30 minutes, then drain and rinse under running water until the water runs clear. Bring a large, heavy saucepan of water to a boil. Add the salt and rice and cook, uncovered, bubbling steadily, for 7 minutes, or until a grain feels almost tender but still has a little bite. Turn the rice into the sieve and rinse under hot running water, then drain well to remove excess salt. Put 2 tablespoons of the oil into the pan with 1 tablespoon water and heat until it steams, then spoon in the rice and cover with the second 2 tablespoons of oil. Wrap a dish towel under the lid of the pan, then place it firmly into position so that you have a perfect seal. Steam the rice over very low heat for 20 minutes. Spoon the rice onto a warm plate, then loosen the crisp layer sticking to the bottom of the pan and stir that into the rice.

SESAME SPICED RICE

SERVES 4
KEEPS FOR 3 DAYS IN THE FRIDGE | FREEZES FOR 3 MONTHS

The addition of a little ground meat simmered in wine gives this rich rice casserole extra body and flavor. It is a perfect dish to serve at a buffet dinner party with cold meat or poultry.

½ cup/2oz/50g sesame seeds

1 tbsp sunflower oil

1 small onion, finely chopped

½lb/225g ground beef

1 cup/7oz/200g basmati or other long-grain rice

⅔ cup/150 ml full-bodied red wine

1 tbsp dark soy sauce

1 tsp paprika

1 tsp salt

1½ cups/350 ml beef or chicken stock

Preheat the oven to 350°F/180°C. Put the sesame seeds on a baking tray and toast in the oven for 10–15 minutes, or until golden brown. Remove.

Meanwhile, gently heat the oil in a Dutch oven or flameproof casserole dish and sauté the onion until soft and golden. Add the meat and cook until it loses its redness and begins to brown, stirring with a fork. Now add the rice and cook until it loses its glassy appearance, stirring well. Pour in the wine and bubble fiercely until its volume is reduced by half. Add the soy sauce, paprika, salt, and stock and bring to a full boil. Stir well and transfer to the oven.

Cook, covered, for 30 minutes until the rice is tender and has absorbed all the liquid. Stir in the toasted sesame seeds.

To reheat from cold, sprinkle the surface lightly with water, cover, then put in a moderate oven at 350°F/180°C for 15 minutes, or until warm. In the microwave, cook covered on 100 percent power for 2–3 minutes. Once cooked, dish can be kept hot in the oven at 300°F/150°C for up to half an hour.

BULGAR PILAF

SERVES 4

KEEPS FOR FOR 2 DAYS IN THE FRIDGE | FREEZES FOR 3 MONTHS

This can be served hot as a light and savory accompaniment, or at room temperature with a cold buffet. It is equally tasty either way.

1 small onion, finely chopped

2 tbsp oil

1 cup/6oz/175g bulgar

1 tsp finely grated
orange zest

1/4 cup/2oz/50g raisins

1 3/4 cups/425 ml chicken stock

salt

ground black pepper

1/4 cup/1oz/25g pine nuts, toasted
in a dry pan

2 tbsp/1oz/25g chopped parsley
(enough to "green" the pilaf)

4 scallions, finely sliced

In an 8–9in/20–23cm heavy-based saucepan or sauté pan, fry the onion in the oil over moderate heat, stirring until softened. Stir in the bulgar and the orange zest and cook the mixture, stirring, for 1 minute. Add the raisins, stock, and salt and pepper to taste, bring the liquid to a boil, and cook, covered, over low heat for 10 minutes, or until the liquid is absorbed.

To serve hot, fluff the pilaf with a fork and stir in the pine nuts, parsley, and scallions. To serve cold, allow the pilaf to cool for 15 minutes before stirring in the remaining ingredients.

This dish reheats well in the microwave—allow 2 minutes in a covered dish on 100 percent (1000W) power, or until piping hot.

TRADITIONAL KASHA

SERVES 6
KEEPS FOR FOR 3 DAYS IN THE FRIDGE | FREEZES FOR 3 MONTHS

Kasha is made from roasted buckwheat grains. You can buy it in health food stores or online.

1 ⅓ cups/8oz/225g kasha (roasted buckwheat)

1 beaten egg

2 cups/425ml boiling water

2 tsp paprika

1 tsp salt

10 grinds of black pepper

1 large onion, finely chopped

3 tbsp chicken fat or margarine

4–5 tbsp leftover beef or chicken gravy (optional, but very good)

Put the uncooked kasha into a large sauté pan and add the beaten egg. Mix well and cook over medium heat for 5 minutes, stirring occasionally, until the groats look puffy and dry. Add the boiling water, paprika, salt, and pepper, then cover and simmer for 15 minutes until the liquid is absorbed.

Meanwhile, in a covered pan, gently sauté the onion in the fat or margarine until soft and golden, then add to the cooked kasha, stirring well. Stir in the gravy, if using, and reheat until steaming. May be reheated.

VARIATION
KASHA VARNISHKES
Cook 1 cup/4oz/115g farfalle. Add it to the kasha just before serving and mix well.

MEAT STOCKS

EACH RECIPE MAKES APPROXIMATELY 5 CUPS/1 L
KEEPS FOR FOR 3 DAYS IN THE FRIDGE | FREEZES FOR 3 MONTHS

Stock is quite simply a flavored liquid from which soups and sauces are made. The more flavorful the stock, the tastier the soup or sauce. In Jewish cooking, meat stocks are traditionally made by simmering the coarser parts of root vegetables with herbs and koshered bones, enriched if desired with a piece of shin beef or a portion of fowl. To extract flavor from these ingredients, the stock must be simmered very slowly for many hours, preferably in the oven. However, with a pressure cooker, you can make excellent stock in just 1 hour. If stock is made the day before cooking the soup, it should be chilled in the fridge—it will then be easy to lift off any fat on the surface. Stock is an excellent way to use up odds and ends of vegetables that have a good flavor but are too coarse to use in other dishes. Here are some different ways to make meat stocks for soup.

CHICKEN STOCK

Next time you roast or braise a chicken, freeze the cooked carcass and you will have the foundation for a low-fat chicken soup that can rival the flavor of one enriched in the traditional way, with a piece of fat hen.

To make the soup, break up the carcass so it will fit comfortably into your soup pot, stock pot, or pressure cooker, add a couple of sets of giblets (omit the livers, since they impair the flavor), 2 fat carrots, the white part of a leek (both finely sliced), a few squishy tomatoes (or 2 teaspoons tomato paste), ½ large onion, and a small bunch of parsley. Add 6¼ cups/1.5l water, 1 teaspoon salt, and 20 grinds of black pepper and allow the pot to simmer on the lowest possible heat for 3 hours (or pressure cook for 1 hour). Better still, simmer it in the oven, where it will develop an even richer flavor.

After cooking, strain out the vegetables, bones, and giblets, returning any chicken salvaged from them to the stock, then refrigerate or freeze overnight so that the fat content will solidify on top and can be easily removed the next day. Or, pour off the fat in batches from the warm, strained stock using a large fat separator. When you are reheating the stock, you can strenghthen the chicken flavor with a couple of chicken bouillon cubes, if necessary.

BEEF BONE STOCK

generous 1 lb/500g koshered beef bones

1 large leek, green part only

leaves from a head of celery

½ white turnip

½ onion

2 squashy tomatoes

1 bay leaf

20 peppercorns

1 large sprig of parsley

2 tsp salt

Using the stove Put all the ingredients into a stock pot, bring to a simmer, then simmer on the stovetop for 3 hours, or transfer to the oven at 300°F/150°C for the same length of time.

In a pressure cooker Put the bones and the coarsely cut vegetables into a pressure cooker and cover with cold water. Add the seasonings. Pressurize for 1 hour.

With either method, strain out all the vegetables. If the stock is not to be used at once, it can be either chilled until the next day or boiled down to concentrate it, then poured into a plastic container and frozen.

BEEF AND BONE STOCK

Proceed as above, but add ½–1 lb/225–450g beef shank to the vegetables. The cooked meat can be served in stock as a soup or used to fill pastries.

Note If a soup requires a long cooking time—for instance, barley soup and split-pea soup—the bones and meat (if using) can be cooked simultaneously with the soup ingredients. In that case, the bones should be put into the pan, covered with the amount of water specified in the recipe, and the mixture brought to a boil. The scum from the bones should then be carefully removed with a wet spoon before the cereals and vegetables are added.

ROAST BEEF BONE STOCK

The bone left from a roast rib of beef makes excellent stock. Proceed as above.

SOUP GARNISHES

KNAIDLACH

MATZO BALLS

SERVES 6–8

KEEPS FOR 2 DAYS IN THE FRIDGE | FREEZES FOR 1 MONTH

These are also sometimes called halkes. The secret of success is to use sufficient fat to make them tender yet still firm when the spoon goes in. Provided the specified amount of fat is used, the quantity of matzo meal may be increased if you prefer a firmer (though equally tender) texture.

2 large eggs

2 very slightly rounded tbsp softened rendered chicken fat, chicken-flavored vegetable fat, or margarine

²/₃–¾ cup/150ml–175ml warm chicken stock, broth, or water, as needed

¼ cup/1oz/25g ground almonds

1 cup/4oz/125g medium matzo meal

¼ tsp white pepper

¼ tsp ground ginger

3 tsp salt

Whisk the eggs until fluffy, then stir in the soft fat, stock or water, ground almonds, matzo meal, white pepper, ginger, and 1 teaspoon salt, and mix thoroughly. The mixture should look moist and thick, but should not be quite firm enough to form into balls. If too soft, add a little more meal; if too firm, add a teaspoon or two of water. Chill for at least an hour, but overnight will do no harm. The mixture will then firm up.

Half-fill a pan with water and bring to a boil, then add the remaining 2 teaspoons of salt. Take pieces of the chilled mixture the size of large walnuts and roll between wetted palms into balls. Drop these balls into the boiling water, reduce the heat until the water is simmering, cover, and simmer for 40 minutes without removing the lid. Strain from the water with a slotted spoon and drop into your simmering soup.

Alternatively, for a small number or a special occasion, cook the knaidlach in chicken stock rather than in water. They will absorb some of the soup and its delicious flavors.

Note To freeze knaidlach, open-freeze the cooked and drained knaidlach until solid—about 2 hours—before transferring them to plastic bags. To use, defrost for 1 hour at room temperature, then reheat in the simmering soup.

BAKED CROÛTONS
TO GARNISH MEAT SOUPS

SERVES 6–8
FREEZES FOR 3 MONTHS

4 large slices brown or rye bread

3 tbsp sunflower or olive oil

1 tsp dried herbes de Provence

Preheat the oven to 350°F/180°C.

Cut the bread into ½in/1cm cubes and mix, in a flat baking pan, with the oil and herbs. Bake for 15–20 minutes, stirring once or twice so that the croûtons brown evenly.

BUTTERED CROÛTONS
TO GARNISH CREAM SOUPS

SERVES 4
LEFTOVERS FREEZE FOR 3 MONTHS

The garnish for a creamy soup must be light yet crisp. Use slightly stale bread to get the best results.

4 thin slices bread

2 tbsp/1oz/25g butter

1 tbsp oil

Cut the bread into ½in/1cm cubes.

To fry Heat the butter and oil in a heavy frying pan. As soon as the foaming stops, put in the bread and fry gently until crisp and golden on all sides. Drain well on crumpled paper towel.

To bake Preheat oven to 350°F/180°C. Melt the butter and oil in a tray about 9 x 7in/23 x 18cm and 1in/2.5cm deep. Add the croûtons, shake well to coat them with the oil, then bake for 15–20 minutes, shaking once, until crisp and golden brown. Drain on crumpled paper.

Reheat briefly in the oven just before serving in little pottery dishes.

SAUCES

TARTAR SAUCE

SERVES 4–6

KEEPS FOR 2 WEEKS IN THE FRIDGE | DO NOT FREEZE

A piquant sauce to serve with grilled, poached, or fried fish such as lemon sole, haddock, plaice, or halibut.

¾ cups/150ml mayonnaise

½ tbsp lemon juice

1 tbsp plain yogurt or fromage frais

1 small pickled cucumber, finely chopped

1 tsp snipped chives

1 tsp chopped tarragon

1 tsp chopped parsley

1 scallion or shallot, chopped

1 pinch of Cayenne pepper

3 stuffed olives, chopped

Mix all the ingredients together. Refrigerate for several hours to allow the flavors to blend.

EASY HOLLANDAISE SAUCE

SERVES 4
MAKE AND EAT ON THE SAME DAY

This way of making this delicious sauce is easy in comparison with the classic method! It is essential that both the liquids and the butter are thoroughly heated before they are added to the egg yolks.

1 tbsp lemon juice

½ tbsp white wine vinegar

1 stick/4oz/125g butter or margarine

2 egg yolks

½ tsp superfine sugar

pinch of salt

Place the lemon juice and vinegar in a small saucepan and heat until bubbling. Heat the butter or margarine in another pan. In the blender or processor, blend the egg yolks, sugar, and salt for 2 seconds. With the machine running, slowly trickle the vinegar mixture into the blender or food processor. Do the same with the foaming butter or margarine, slowly trickling it in until you have a thick, smooth sauce. Keep warm, if desired, in a heatproof bowl standing in a pan of warm water.

VARIATIONS

SAUCE BÉARNAISE
Stir in 1½ tablespoons chopped tarragon or 1 teaspoon of dried tarragon after the butter or margarine has been added.

AVOCADO HOLLANDAISE
Peel 1 small, very ripe avocado and remove the pit. Mash or purée the flesh in a food processor, then remove. There is no need to wash the bowl. Make the sauce as above, then pulse or mix in the avocado purée.

DOUGHS, BATTERS, AND PASTRY

KUCHEN DOUGH

MAKES 1 LARGE LOAF
KEEPS FOR 2 DAYS IN THE FRIDGE | UNRISEN DOUGH FREEZES FOR 3 MONTHS;
SHAPED BUT UNBAKED CAKES 2 WEEKS; BAKED CAKES 3 MONTHS

1 egg

1 1/2 tbsp cold milk

hot water

1/4 cake/1/2oz/14g fresh yeast or
2 tsp/1/4oz/7g instant yeast

2 cups/8oz/225g all-purpose flour

1/2 tsp salt

1/4 cup/1 1/2oz/40g superfine sugar

3 tbsp/1 1/2oz/40g soft butter or
margarine

zest of 1 lemon

oil, for greasing (optional)

Break the egg into a measuring cup, add the cold milk, whisk to blend, then make up to 2/3 cup/150ml with hot water. If you are using fresh yeast, add to the liquid and stir until dissolved. If you are using instant yeast, combine it with the flour, salt, and sugar into the bowl of your mixer and mix thoroughly. Add the liquid, butter or margarine, and the lemon zest and beat for about 5 minutes until the dough is smooth and stretchy and leaves the bowl and the beater clean when pulled away. If too sticky, add a further 1–2 tablespoons of flour—the dough should be firm enough to form into a soft ball.

To rise and bake the same day Turn the dough onto a pastry board and knead for a few seconds—you will now have a satiny ball of dough. Grease a mixing bowl very lightly with oil, turn the dough in it to coat it, then leave it in the bowl and cover with plastic wrap. It will take about 1 1/2 hours in the kitchen to double in bulk. Then press the dough down, turn it over, and knead it in the bowl for 1–2 minutes— this evenly distributes the gas bubbles in the dough.

To rise overnight Slip the dough into a greased plastic bag large enough to allow it to double in volume. Tie loosely and put on the bottom shelf of the fridge. Before using the dough the next day, allow it to return to room temperature for 1 hour (you can hasten the process by putting it in the microwave on defrost for 2 minutes). Knead for a further 1–2 minutes as above.

In either case, set the dough aside while you prepare your desired filling (see pages 144 and 145).

QUICK KUCHEN BATTER

Quick kuchen is a general term to cover a wide range of cakes that can be topped either with sweet crumbles (usually called streusels) or with an assortment of seasonal fruits (see page 150). These cakes do not have the same flavor or texture as a yeast-raised kuchen, but they are still delicious.

¾ cup/4oz/115g cake flour

¾ cup/4oz/115g all-purpose flour

2 tsp baking powder

6 tbsp/3oz/75g soft butter

⅔ cup/4oz/125g superfine sugar

1 large egg

⅔ cup/150 ml milk, or ½ cup/125ml if using a food processor

Put all the ingredients into a bowl or food processor and mix by hand or machine until a thick, smooth batter is formed— 15 seconds by food processor, 2–3 minutes by hand or electric mixer.

Oil either a rectangular cake pan measuring 12 x 9 x 2in/30 x 23 x 5cm or a 9in/23cm round or square pan of a similar depth. Spoon the batter into the chosen pan and level the top. The kuchen is now ready to be used.

CHEESECAKE PASTRY CRUST

LINES A 9–10IN/23–25CM LOOSE-BOTTOMED TART PAN ABOUT 1¼IN/3CM DEEP OR AN 8IN/20CM PIE PAN WITH SLOPING SIDES, ABOUT 2IN/5CM DEEP
KEEPS IN THE FRIDGE FOR 2 DAYS | FREEZES FOR 3 MONTHS

⅔ cup/3oz/85g all-purpose flour, plus extra for dusting

⅔ cup/3oz/85g cake flour

1 tsp baking powder

1 stick/4oz/125g butter or margarine

½ cup/2oz/50g confectioner's sugar

1 egg yolk (reserve the white for the filling, see traditional cheesecake, page 146)

1 tbsp water

Put all the ingredients into a bowl and work together with a wooden spoon until a dough is formed. Chill for 30 minutes.

Roll out the pastry on a lightly floured board to fit the chosen pan, easing it in gently so as not to stretch it. Chill again while you prepare the filling.

ADAPTING RECIPES FOR THE KOSHER KITCHEN

Many recipes need adapting in some way before they can be used in the Jewish kitchen: they may contain non-kosher ingredients, or combine meat and dairy products in the same dish, or simply include dairy in a dish that is to be served as part of a meat meal. It is then a question of finding suitable alternative ingredients that, while satisfying the requirements of the dietary laws, will not radically alter the flavor and texture of the original dish. Here are suggestions for overcoming the common problems of five key ingredients.

Butter

- To fry meat and poultry, substitute 2 tbsp olive or sunflower oil or chicken-flavored vegetable fat for each 2 tbsp/1oz/30g butter.
- To sauté vegetables for a meat casserole or soup, substitute an equal amount of margarine or olive oil.
- To fry or roast potatoes, substitute 2 tbsp of oil and a scant 1 tbsp/½oz/15g margarine for each 2 tbsp/1oz/30g butter.
- In a sponge pudding or cake for a meat meal, substitute an equal amount of soft margarine; in addition, use water to mix instead of milk. If only a small number of eggs is included in the recipe, substitute an extra egg for 3½ tbsp of the milk.
- In pastry for a meat meal, substitute ½ cup/4oz/125g margarine and 2 tbsp/1oz/25g soft shortening for each 10 tbsp/5oz/150g butter.
- In crêpe batter with a meat meal, substitute an equal amount of melted margarine for sweet crêpes, or sunflower oil for savory.
- In sauces or soups that contain chicken stock, substitute an equal quantity of chicken-flavored vegetable fat or margarine.
- To fry pancakes or crêpes for a meat meal, substitute a flavorless vegetable oil.
- To shallow-fry blintzes for a meat meal, use an equal quantity of margarine plus 1 tbsp flavorless (e.g. sunflower) oil to prevent over-browning of the margarine.

Milk

- In a batter for crêpes, blintzes, pancakes, or popovers to serve with a meat meal, substitute a scant 1 cup/225ml water plus 1 egg and 1 tbsp of flavorless oil for each 1 cup/275ml milk. The blintzes and pancakes will be lighter and thinner, and fried stuffed blintzes will be crisper than when made with milk. Popovers will have a crisper crust, but they will be a less spongy inside.
- In sauces or soups that contain chicken or meat, or to serve with a meat meal, substitute either kosher non-dairy cream or chicken stock, making the soup look "creamy" by whisking in 1 egg yolk for each $^2/_3$ cup/150ml of liquid, then heating until steaming.

Cream

- To enrich a chicken sauce, soup, or casserole, either substitute an equal quantity of unsweetened kosher non-dairy pouring cream (not whipping cream) or thicken the sauce with 1 egg yolk for each 2–3 tbsp of cream. Refrigerate to allow the cream to thicken.
- For whipped cream in a cold dessert, replace each $^2/_3$ cup/150ml of heavy or whipping cream with $^1/_2$ cup/125ml of kosher non-dairy whipping cream or, in a gelatine dessert, for every $^2/_3$ cup/150ml of heavy or whipping cream, use a meringue made by whisking 2 egg whites until stiff and then whisking in 2 tsp of superfine sugar—this will produce a lighter texture than cream.

Chicken Stock

- In a milk soup or sauce, substitute vegetable stock made with a cube or concentrate or a chicken-flavored parev bouillon cube or powder.

Shellfish

- In a fish cocktail or salad, substitute an equal weight of fillets of firm white fish such as halibut, bream, or lemon sole, poached, then cut into small cubes or coarsely flaked.
- In a creamy casserole, filling for pastry, or fish pie, substitute an equal quantity of fresh salmon, halibut, or haddock, poached, then flaked or cut in 1 in/2.5cm cubes.
- In a deep-fried dish, substitute an equal weight of raw fillets of lemon sole, plaice, or baby halibut, cut into bite-size strips. Coat with batter or with flour, egg, and breadcrumbs and fry as directed.

INDEX

Thus sayeth Kohelet, "There is nothing new under the sun," and of no sphere is this aphorism from Ecclesiastes more true than the world of food and cooking. My own knowledge is only the sum of that accumulated by hundreds of generations of Jewish women who have cooked before me. All I can hope to do is to make that knowledge relevant—and accessible—to people cooking at this particular time.

I must pay tribute to those women who cooked before me and who, without benefit of cookbooks, established an oral tradition of superb Jewish food that has been passed down in an unbroken chain from mother to daughter—and not infrequently to son—from the beginning of our recorded history.

Evelyn Rose

PUBLISHER'S ACKNOWLEDGMENTS

Each recipe in this book is the outcome not only of exhaustive research and recipe testing on the part of Evelyn Rose, but of the generations of Jewish cooks, past and present, who informed and inspired her work.

In particular, the publisher would like to thank Judi and David Rose for their support and advice, consultant Richard Erlich, photographer Clare Winfield, prop stylist Wei Tang, and food stylist Jayne Cross.

First American edition published in 2016 by

INTERLINK BOOKS
An imprint of Interlink Publishing Group, Inc.
46 Crosby Street
Northampton, Massachusetts 01060
www.interlinkbooks.com

Library of Congress Cataloging-in-Publication Data available

ISBN 978-1-56656-073-3

10 9 8 7 6 5 4 3 2 1

Commissioning editor: Emily Preece-Morrison
American edition editor: Leyla Moushabeck
Photographer: Clare Winfield
Design concept: Laura Russell
Design layout: Gail Jones
Cover design: Leyla Moushabeck
Prop stylist: Wei Tang
Proofreaders: Wendy Hobson

Reproduction by: COLOURDEPTH
Printed and bound by: Toppan Leefung Printing Ltd, China